W9-BDU-244

FRANK LLOYD WRIGHT

Preserving an Architectural Heritage

Decorative Designs from The Domino's Pizza Collection

Frank Lloyd Wright at Taliesin East,
Spring Green, Wisconsin, 1937.

FRANK LLOYD WRIGHT

Preserving an Architectural Heritage

Decorative Designs from The Domino's Pizza Collection

DAVID A. HANKS

E. P. Dutton   New York

Book design by Elizabeth Finger
Typeset by Michael and Winifred Bixler

Copyright © 1989 by David A. Hanks.
All rights reserved.
No part of this publication may be reproduced or
transmitted in any form or by any means,
electronic or mechanical, including photocopy,
recording, or any information storage and
retrieval system now known or to be invented,
without permission in writing from the publisher,
except by a reviewer who wishes to quote brief
passages in connection with a review written for
inclusion in a magazine, newspaper, or broadcast.
Published in the United States by E. P. Dutton,
a division of Penguin Books USA Inc.,
2 Park Avenue, New York, N.Y. 10016.
Published simultaneously in Canada by
Fitzhenry and Whiteside, Limited, Toronto.
Library of Congress
Catalog Card Number: 89–50249.
Printed and bound by
Dai Nippon Printing Co., Ltd., Tokyo, Japan.
ISBN: 0–525–24522–7 (cloth);
ISBN: 0–525–48296–2 (DP).
10 9 8 7 6 5 4 3 2 1 First Edition

PARTICIPATING MUSEUMS

Seattle Art Museum

Chicago Historical Society

Albright-Knox Art Gallery

The Denver Art Museum

The Pennsylvania Academy of the Fine Arts

Dallas Museum of Art

Exhibition organized by the Smithsonian Institution Traveling Exhibition Service and David A. Hanks and Associates, Inc., in cooperation with The National Center for the Study of Frank Lloyd Wright.

TABLE OF CONTENTS

My interest in Frank Lloyd Wright began at the age of twelve, when I discovered a book about this important American architect in the Traverse City, Michigan, library containing illustrations of the Robie house, Fallingwater, the Johnson Wax building, and others. It was hard to believe that a single individual had designed all of these buildings as each was so different. My passion for Wright's designs had begun, and it became stronger as my knowledge of the architect's ideas and his work grew.

At seventeen, I moved to Ann Arbor where I saw and admired Wright's houses in the area, especially the William Palmer residence that was designed in 1950. Later, while stationed in Japan, I visited the Imperial Hotel in Tokyo at every opportunity. Although I was never able to see the guest rooms, I managed to explore the rest of the hotel and thus discovered the splendors of its vast architectural spaces as well as the intricate details of its elaborate ornament and furnishings.

In the early 1970s, I embarked on a wider tour of Wright houses in Illinois, Michigan, and Minnesota, which strengthened my conviction of the importance of Wright's organic architecture. I decided that the new headquarters for Domino's Pizza should reflect Wright's principles as seen in his Prairie houses. The Prairie house, with its timeless, classic beauty, is my personal favorite because its eye-pleasing lines complement the existing landscape, avoiding unnatural or harsh contrasts to the natural environment. I wanted to build Prairie-style buildings that conform to the landscape, and I intended to complete a dream that Wright had never realized: to merge technology and nature by building a skyscraper in a rural setting. In Gunnar Birkerts I found an architect who was willing to carry out these ideas. Birkerts's low, Wright-style office buildings for Domino's Pizza are in a pastoral setting that incorporates a farm and a lake. My initial idea was to re-create "The Golden Beacon" tower that was conceived by Wright in 1957 for a site on Chicago's Gold Coast, but was never constructed. Instead, Gunnar Birkerts has designed a contemporary thirty-story office tower and convention center that will convey Wright's ideas. The first of three phases of what will be a six-tenth-of-a-mile-long building was completed in 1985. Domino's Farms is an exciting concept for a corporation and attracts over 850,000 visitors annually.

Although my desire to collect the designs of Frank Lloyd Wright began as a personal interest, I slowly came to realize that a greater purpose exists for the growing collection. I am exhilarated, yet overwhelmed, by the awesome task of preserving the works of Frank Lloyd Wright in the hope that future generations of his admirers will learn about his architecture and develop a deeper appreciation of his contributions to our American heritage. Toward this end we have established The National Center for the Study of Frank Lloyd Wright where students, scholars, and the general public may come to obtain information about Wright's work. This is now a major repository for Wright's drawings, archives, and decorative designs.

The National Center includes the collection of Wright-designed artifacts—some of his finest designs—that are also available both to scholars and the general public. In some instances an architectural element by Wright is all that survives from buildings that have been demolished. We do not remove objects from existing Wright structures and we attempt to encourage the preservation of Wright's architecture *in situ*.

I sometimes feel that the spirit of Frank Lloyd Wright is looking approvingly over my shoulder as I struggle to preserve every example of his designs that I can. I feel that I am blessed with the opportunity to keep his work alive and accessible to future generations for their study and appreciation.

THOMAS S. MONAGHAN

Detail of the exterior of the Domino's Pizza World Headquarters.

Thomas S. Monaghan, Founder and
President of Domino's Pizza, Inc., in
The National Center for the Study of
Frank Lloyd Wright, Ann Arbor,
Michigan, 1988.

ACKNOWLEDGMENTS

The preparation of this book could not have been accomplished without the considerable efforts of many people. At The National Center for the Study of Frank Lloyd Wright we wish to acknowledge Rosemary Buku, Kathryn Crawley, Toni J. Hendrix, Darwin C. Matthews, Lisa A. Smith, Ray Wetzel, and Jeff Stout. At the Smithsonian Institution Traveling Exhibition Service we are indebted to the following: Betty Teller, the exhibition coordinator; her assistant, Penni Billet; and Mary Dillon, exhibit designer. Also at SITES we would like to thank Anna Cohn, Director; Deborah Bennett, Public Relations Director; Myriam Springuel, Education Director; and Andrea Stevens, Publications Director. We wish also to acknowledge the work of John Meehan and Jean Quinette at the office of Smithsonian Telecommunications for their work on the film created to accompany the exhibition. In the office of David A. Hanks & Associates, we wish to acknowledge the efforts of Charles Buckley, Kate Carmel, Diane Charbonneau, Desiree Cossette, Ellen Davidson, Mary Dellin, Dick Goodbody, Marc Rabun, Caroline Stern, and Jennifer Toher Teulié.

The book could not have been completed without the diligent work of Cyril I. Nelson, editor at E.P. Dutton, and the design provided by Elizabeth Finger.

Many others have been invaluable in their support of this publication, including the Domino's Pizza Preservation Committee: Sonia Cooke, Donald Kalec, and Carla Lind.

S.A.B./D.A.H.

The photographs of the Chicago Architectural Photographic Company are part of a collection of over 200 glass negatives owned by The National Center for the Study of Frank Lloyd Wright. These were largely the work of photographer E. Fuermann, and they concentrate on Wright's buildings from the 1890s through the 1920s.

INTRODUCTION

Collecting vs. Preservation of
Frank Lloyd Wright's
Decorative Designs

To Wright, "organic" architecture embodied designing furnishings that would be integral to the structures that he planned according to this principle. In an English preface to the *Ausgeführte Bauten und Entwürfe*, published in Germany in 1910, he wrote: "In Organic Architecture then, it is quite impossible to consider the building as one thing, its furnishings another and its setting and environment still another. The Spirit in which these buildings are conceived sees all these together at work as one thing. All are to be studiously foreseen and provided for in the nature of the structure. All these should become mere details of the character and completeness of the structure. . . . The very chairs and tables, cabinets and even musical instruments, where practicable, are of the building itself, never fixtures upon it. . . ."

Thus, preserving Wright's architecture, it would appear, should entail preserving as completely as possible the "organic" unity of his interiors. The traditional approach to architectural preservation, especially in the United States, has tended to focus to a greater extent on the exterior of a building. In Wright's case, the very popularity of his interiors and decorative designs has encouraged dismantling and dispersal. Ironically, both private and museum collecting, normally a means of preserving significant works of art, have now become the cause of the dissemination of many of Wright's works.

Other thorny questions also present themselves: For example, should Wright's houses be looked upon as "museums," or can they be adapted for contemporary living? Can the furniture designed by Wright early in this century function satisfactorily for present-day occupants of a Wright house? What would Wright himself advocate? It is known that his aesthetic evolved, and when renovating or "modernizing" earlier interiors, he often changed the design. The architect's own philosophy would have precluded preserving his houses and interiors as "museums" frozen in time. Wright believed his interiors were to be lived in and experienced.

The Domino's Pizza Collection of Wright's decorative designs must be considered in light of the many questions that arise in connection with his architecture. It should also be seen as part of a much larger and ongoing program initiated in 1984 by Domino's Pizza to preserve Wright's architecture *in situ*, as well as to educate the public through the display and elucidation of his decorative work.

The phenomenon whereby interiors and other architectural settings are removed from their original context is not unique to Frank Lloyd Wright, as it has occurred repeatedly. A 1987 article in *The New York Times* about The Metropolitan Museum of Art's exhibition of paintings by Francisco de Zurbaran (1598–1664) could aptly describe any exhibition of Wright's decorative designs: "Almost all the major works in the show were made for architectural contexts in which they can no longer be seen." The Spanish monasteries that had provided the setting for Zurbaran's religious paintings seem remote to us today, but they were once as integral to Zurbaran's work as a Wright house is to its original furnishings. Yet when the architecture of our own century is disseminated, marketed, and collected, historians and preservationists express alarm and concern. The removal of Wright furnishings from the interiors for which they were designed actually began at a surprisingly early date—in fact, during his Prairie period. The earliest instance may have been in 1908 when Francis W. Little sold the Peoria, Illinois, house that Wright had designed six years earlier and took with him some of the original furnishings, including wall sconces, to Northome, the new Minnesota house that Wright built for Little in 1912. Wright may have objected more to the addition of the earlier furniture to his new design than to the fact that it had been removed from the Peoria house. His designs had undergone remarkable changes in those ten years and, presumably, he could have created a more unified interior

View of the exhibition gallery in
The National Center for the Study of
Frank Lloyd Wright.

without including his client's earlier furniture and decorative accessories. Yet evidence of this somewhat uncomfortable compromise between architect and client survives in archival photographs of the Little living room, and it may be seen even now in its present installation in The Metropolitan Museum of Art in New York City.

In fact, most of the furnishings that Wright designed to be integral to his Prairie houses were removed by either the original owners or by later ones, and the interiors were modified to suit contemporary taste and functional considerations. It was not unusual for original clients of a Wright house to take furnishings with them when they sold the house. Thus these interiors, in terms of being the unified entities that Wright intended, had already been compromised. By the 1950s, Prairie houses retaining any of the original furnishings were notable exceptions, and seldom was an appreciation and understanding of Wright's organic principles inherited by succeeding generations of owners.

Throughout much of this century, Wright's decorative designs and interiors were not held in anything like the high regard that prevails now. As recently as the early 1970s, Wright furnishings, which in today's market command astronomical prices, were sometimes simply discarded or relegated to storage by more recent owners of Wright houses. For example, a later owner of the 1908 Meyer May house in Grand Rapids, Michigan, went so far as to chop up the magnificent dining table and lamps, incorporating some of the pieces in a box built for storing firewood. Also, the dining table of the William G. Fricke house in Oak Park, Illinois, which is now in the Victoria & Albert Museum in London, was once used as a basement work table.

In contrast, through a number of successful sales of Wright's work by Christie's New York, the early 1980s saw increased appreciation of the importance of Wright's decorative designs. This sudden and dramatic surge of interest in Wright's work provided the owners of Wright's houses with an unpleasant dilemma. In addition to being burdened with rising costs for restoration and maintenance, they had to insure at escalating valuations windows, furniture, and other surviving artifacts. On one hand, because of the lure of rising prices, Wright's decorative designs were no longer destroyed; on the other, a growing number of Wright homeowners took advantage of the financial rewards of consigning windows and furnishings to auction houses or to dealers. Inevitably, their actions further violated the architectural unity and integrity of Wright's structures.

In May 1982, Christie's New York held its first sale of Wright-designed furniture and windows. In some instances, the consignors to the sale were descendants of the original clients who had removed Wright's furnishings when they sold their houses. This sale featured examples of windows and furniture, as well as smaller objects designed not only by Wright but also by such contemporaries as Greene and Greene, whose work had suffered neglect and is now of ever-increasing interest to museums and private collectors. The record prices realized by Christie's at this sale and at subsequent architectural sales had previously been attained only by works of decorative art of earlier periods. Museums and collectors in the United States and Europe now were competing for the remnants of architecture and interior designs by Wright and his contemporaries.

Another factor also played its part in this perplexing situation. During the 1980s, museums focused public attention on the aesthetic quality of Wright's decorative designs. Indeed, by 1980, The Metropolitan Museum of Art had assumed a leading role in collecting Wright's designs removed from their original architectural context. The Metropolitan's extensive collection of Wright's work began as early as 1967, when the triptych of windows from the Avery Coonley Playhouse of 1912, a highly important work, was acquired. In 1972, the museum acquired an entire Wright room, the aforementioned

Francis Little living room designed in 1912. This room stands as the culmination of the historic settings in the Metropolitan's American Wing, which range in date from the seventeenth to the twentieth century. Installed in 1982, the living room includes furnishings original to both Francis Little's Peoria house from 1903 and the 1912 Minnesota house.

To what extent the Metropolitan Museum's acquisition of the Little room, along with other examples of Wright's decorative designs, can be considered a preservation effort depends to a great extent on one's point of view and circumstances. The metal furniture from the 1904 Larkin Company Administration Building in Buffalo, New York, in the museum's collection is from a demolished structure; therefore, its acquisition in 1979 and subsequent exhibition at the museum can be considered a preservation effort. These furnishings are among a small group of the only three-dimensional artifacts to survive the destruction of the building in 1950, and they give a sense of the very presence and integrity of the original building that are now brought to life only through black-and-white photographs.

The acquisition of the interiors from the Little house might be considered an act of vandalism were it not for the fact that this important structure was about to be demolished. The Metropolitan's intervention became an act of preservation, thus saving the interiors for posterity. The Little interiors are now divided among several collections; for instance, the library is installed in the Allentown Art Museum, and the bedroom wing is now in the Domino's Pizza Collection, where it awaits installation in a new museum complex.

Wright saw museums as an appropriate setting for his work, and was involved in museum installations of it. In addition, the architect himself played a role in changing his organic units and encouraging the exhibition of his designs apart from the architectural setting to which they were once integral. He was involved in installing an exhibition of his own work at The Art Institute of Chicago as early as 1902, as well as at other museums later on. In 1947, Wright gave two chairs, which he had designed for the Larkin Building and had been using in his own residence, to The Museum of Modern Art in New York City. Perhaps, he believed that in a museum context his designs would be compared favorably to those of his contemporaries.

Clearly, not every museum acquisition can be considered an act of preservation of Wright's work. In 1974, a number of museums purchased from a prominent New York dealer windows that had been removed from the Darwin D. Martin house in Buffalo, New York, although this house was later converted to a museum by the State University of New York.

The issue of the role of museums in preserving Wright's decorative designs has yet to be resolved. On the one hand, removing any of the original furnishings and fittings from Wright's structures obviously compromises their architectural integrity, yet the realities of private ownership make the preservation of Wright's interiors as originally planned an unobtainable ideal. Also, acquiring significant works of art and architecture from any period in order to preserve them has long been considered a responsible function of museums. The presence, therefore, of furniture, windows, and other examples of Wright's decorative work in museums may be preferable to their dispersement through auction sales and the art market in general.

Wright's architecture, of course, must be preserved whenever possible in its physical setting. In recent years, efforts to preserve his architecture *in situ* have grown simultaneously with the desire to collect his decorative designs. Ironically, Wright's buildings often become more valuable in fragmentary form than in their complete state. The Ward Willits residence, which Wright designed in 1901, provides an example of this contradiction. The

Willits house was on an Illinois state preservation register that prohibited major alterations, such as gutting rooms or removing windows. In 1983, the house was offered for sale at $450,000; paradoxically, the windows alone, had they been removed and sold separately, might well have sold for over a million dollars. Without the windows, the integrity of the architecture would have been severely compromised. Clear glass would not have been an acceptable substitute for the patterned screen of art glass that helped define the interior space. A compromise was reached to replace the original windows with exact reproductions, rather than with clear plate glass. The original windows, meanwhile, were given by the owner to the Chicago Historical Society.

Perhaps a more urgent consideration than the furnishings is the preservation of Wright's architectural spaces, the system of art-glass windows, and the return to original exterior and interior paint colors. The stucco that is often seen today as "white" was originally painted in colors that harmonized with the wood trim rather than contrasting with it. High auction prices may account for the removal of art-glass windows and furniture, but Wright's architectural integrity was no less diminished by later structural additions and alterations for contemporary living. A possible compromise, already seen in the case of the Willits house, is to make available reproductions of the original glass and furnishings for private owners of Wright-designed houses and Wright house museums.

For the privately owned Wright house, there is often no legal protection for the interiors and furnishings. The private Wright house is the core of Wright's architecture and demands preservation, yet how this is to be achieved is difficult to determine.

Nor are publicly maintained Wright structures always preserved intact. In 1969, when the Frederick Robie house, dating from 1908, was renovated by the University of Chicago for use as the Adlai F. Stevenson Institute of International Affairs, the architectural firm that was employed—Skidmore, Owings and Merrill—adapted this important interior for contemporary use. Most of the surviving Robie furniture that had been designed by Wright was stored elsewhere. Since this house, which represents the culmination of Wright's Prairie period, was almost demolished in 1957, its very preservation was considered a victory. However, thirty years later, with the growing appreciation of Wright's decorative designs, many feel that the Robie interiors should be restored so that the house will convey Wright's original unified vision—certainly not an impossible task as both the house and its original furnishings belong to the university.

Fortunately, through public and private efforts, a number of Wright's best houses are being preserved *in situ* as museums. The state of Illinois, for example, has preserved in Springfield the important Susan Lawrence Dana house of 1903 (now designated the Dana-Thomas house). For a Wright Prairie house to survive until 1981 with its original furnishings intact is most unusual. In 1981, the Dana-Thomas house was up for sale. As with the Willits house, the Dana windows and furniture, some of Wright's richest and most beautiful designs, would be far more valuable if removed from the house itself, but this would have seriously impaired one of Wright's finest interiors. Only through intervention by the governor of Illinois, James Thompson, was the state able to preserve the house and its furnishings intact. The Dana-Thomas house is now open to the public as a museum, thus giving the visitor a wonderfully accurate sense of a totally unified interior created by Wright. Another highly successful effort was undertaken in 1986 by an American corporation, Steelcase, Inc. The outstanding restoration of Wright's Meyer May house (1909) in Grand Rapids, Michigan, Steelcase's home city, includes both exterior and interior architecture. Original furnishings were located and purchased and reproductions were made when needed. This house, restored as a museum, is now open to the public.

Exterior of the Domino's Pizza
World Headquarters, Ann Arbor,
Michigan, designed by Gunnar Birkerts,
1984.

Exterior of the Snowflake House,
designed for Carlton D. Wall, Plymouth,
Michigan, 1941.

The most ambitious corporate program to preserve Wright's architectural heritage, however, is being undertaken by Domino's Pizza, Inc. In 1986, Thomas S. Monaghan, founder and president of the company, established The National Center for the Study of Frank Lloyd Wright at his corporate headquarters in Ann Arbor, Michigan. Its primary goal is to enhance the appreciation and understanding of Wright's architecture and preserve his work for future generations. Monaghan believed that the public should have access to Wright's architecture, and therefore he established a museum and gallery with this end in view. In addition, Monaghan's program seeks to preserve Wright houses in their original location, as well as the assembling of a major collection of decorative designs, drawings, and archives as part of the Ann Arbor study center.

As recently as 1983, Domino's Pizza acquired its first Wright building: the Snowflake House in Plymouth, Michigan, originally designed by Wright in 1941 for Carlton David Wall and now undergoing restoration. A year later a second architectural work was acquired. This was the disassembled 1,700-square-foot, two-bedroom Usonian Exhibition House and Pavilion, which Wright designed in 1953. A section of the 1953 exhibition called "60 Years of Living Architecture" held on the site of what is now the Guggenheim Museum in New York, this building was important in bringing Wright's concepts of

Usonian architecture to the public. For thirty years, scholars were unable to examine this structure, as it had been dismantled and stored by a former Wright apprentice. Reconstruction of this house on a site at Domino's Farms is part of the plans of the National Center. In 1986, a third architectural work was acquired—the bedroom wing of the Francis Little Minnesota house.

However, the Domino's Pizza Collection, which is the most extensive in the world, is best known for the high quality of the individual objects in the collection. The objects have stimulated both public interest and criticism because of the extraordinary prices Monaghan has paid to acquire them. The Domino's Pizza Collection brings together objects of the highest aesthetic quality ranging from the early years of Wright's career to the end of his life. Among others it includes the dining-room ensemble from the 1899 Joseph Husser house that was demolished in 1924; a side chair from the 1902 Ward Willits house that was removed in the 1950s; and a series of thirty-four windows from the 1912 Avery Coonley Playhouse. These windows, a remarkable ensemble originally removed from the playhouse around 1967, are happily preserved as a most important unit in the collection, rather than having been dispersed to collectors and museums around the world. Although the collection focuses on Wright's masterpieces in decorative designs, it is also encyclopedic, including examples from a variety of structures for study purposes. In addition, the work of Wright's contemporaries and influential predecessors are also represented in the collection so as to provide a broader context in which his work can be seen. Although the collection is part of a larger program to preserve Wright's architectural heritage, clearly there is no question that Monaghan's purchase of individual objects at record-breaking prices encourages their removal from their original architectural setting. To counteract this trend, Domino's Pizza has developed and adopted collecting guidelines, stated in the Appendix, that, if followed by museums, dealers, and auction houses, will help preserve Wright's interior and exterior architecture.

A program of great importance for the future encourages preservation of Wright buildings open to the public. This is being accomplished through the Domino's Pizza preservation program. A challenge grant is awarded annually to Wright buildings in need of restoration or preservation. The first grant was awarded in 1987 to Unity Temple in Oak Park, Illinois, to restore the art-glass windows that play such an important iconographic role in the church. In the same year, the committee cited four other Wright house museums urgently in need of restoration assistance: the Frank Lloyd Wright Home and Studio (1889–1895) in Oak Park and three Los Angeles houses: Hollyhock House (1920), the Charles Ennis house (1923), and the Freeman house (1923). The 1988 grant was awarded to help restore the Samuel Freeman house. The Domino's Pizza Preservation Committee, which consists of a panel of experts and scholars, advises Monaghan on other preservation issues as well, such as possible conflicts between his corporate collecting and his interest in preservation. The committee also recommends loans from the collection to Wright houses that qualify as museums.

This catalogue explores in detail each of the major pieces now in the Domino's Pizza Collection, and attempts to make known the unusual ethical difficulties that collecting presents, and how, ultimately, Wright's architectural heritage can best be preserved. With a renewed consciousness and awareness of the complexities and contradictions discussed, it should be possible to undertake a rational plan of preservation in which museums, collectors, dealers, and owners of Wright's houses can join in a united effort.

DAVID A. HANKS

NATHAN G. MOORE HOUSE

Oak Park, Illinois, 1895

At the request of the client, the original Moore house was English Tudor in style. According to Wright, "Mr. Moore, who was a lawyer and a very sensitive, reputable gentleman, came to me for a house and said he didn't want anything like that Winslow house so that he would have to go around back ways to the train to avoid being laughed at . . ." After a 1922 fire, the house was rebuilt above the first floor. These gates were designed for the original house and are Gothic in character but are stylized so that they are highly abstract, presumably pleasing the client's Gothic taste as well as the architect's geometric sensibility. These gates were originally placed between the main house and the stables. Wright's designs for wrought-iron gates include those for the Francis Apartments of the same year and continued throughout his career, the most recent being those designed for the Lovness house (c. 1956), which are also in the Domino's Pizza Collection.

Exterior of the Nathan G. Moore house, Oak Park, Illinois, 1895.

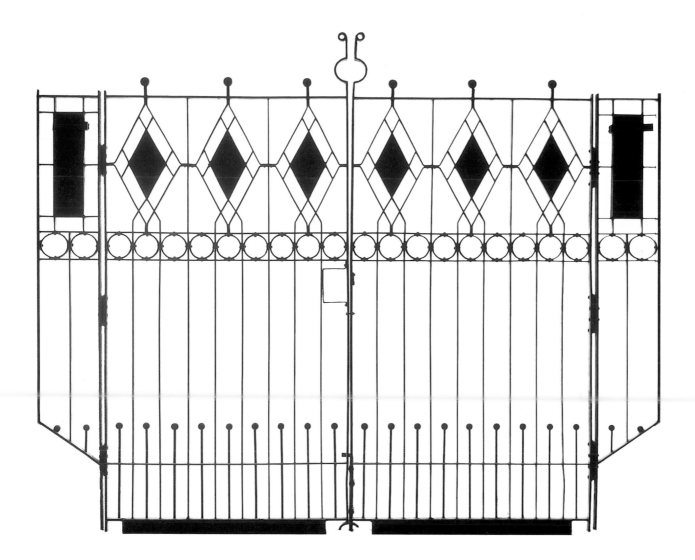

Pair of gates

Wrought iron, painted black
Designed for the Nathan G. Moore house, Oak Park, Illinois
c. 1895
Each section: 74 x 45½ inches (188 x 114.3 cm)
1988.05.01a,b

WRIGHT HOME AND STUDIO

Oak Park, Illinois, 1895–1900

This vase, probably designed in the late 1890s at the start of Wright's independent practice, was featured in some of Wright's early interiors, including the octagonal library in Wright's Oak Park studio and the interior of the Susan Lawrence Dana house. This vase, or weed holder as it is often called, is one of a pair and may have been shown in the 1902 exhibition of Wright's work at The Art Institute of Chicago, which was sponsored by the Chicago Architectural Club. In the archival view two vases flank the armchair designed by the architect for his own house and studio.

As a charter member of the Chicago Arts and Crafts Society, which was founded in 1897, Wright was a major figure in the Arts and Crafts movement in that city. He saw the movement as a means of stimulating dialogue between designers and manufacturers to improve the quality of commercial design, then at a low point and unsuitable for architect-designed interiors. In this example, the material itself as well as the simple lines of its design recall contemporary hand-wrought metal objects that are so typical of this movement. The dark patina harmonized with the fumed oak furniture and woodwork of Wright's early interiors. The use of copper sheet-metal was experimental and amenable to machine production. The vase, probably made by the James A. Miller and Brother Company, a Chicago firm of roofers in slate, tin, and iron, is a variation on a theme that Wright had already explored in drawings that date from the 1890s. In two such drawings, now in the Archives of The Frank Lloyd Wright Foundation, Taliesin West, Wright combined the long shaft and geometric pedestal of the vase with the round form of the copper urn. Wright was apparently fond of this design, for he used it in a number of his Prairie interiors, and in 1955 made a variation of it in wood to accompany the Heritage-Henredon line of furniture.

PRESERVATION NOTE

As small objects representing the architect's work, these copper vases have been sought by museums and collectors. Unfortunately, no "weed holder" remains in the interior for which it was designed, and in fact, most examples were removed at an early date. As noted above, this vase is one of a pair. They may originally have been owned by James A. Miller's brother, Robert Miller, who subsequently gave them to the Third Unitarian Church, Oak Park, from which they were acquired for the Domino's Pizza Collection. Because of polishing, which was never part of Wright's aesthetic intention, the original dark patina had been removed. Restoration of the patinated surface by Hermes Knauer was completed in 1987.

Illustration from the catalogue for an exhibition organized by the Chicago Architectural Club, The Art Institute of Chicago, 1902.

Vase

Sheet copper
Designed 1895–1900 and probably made for the
Wright Home and Studio, Oak Park, Illinois
28 x 4¼ x 4¼ inches (71.1 x 10.9 x 10.9 cm)
1986.26.01

ISIDORE H. HELLER HOUSE

Chicago, Illinois, 1897

The narrow plan of the Heller house conforms to a city lot on Chicago's south side. The third story combines an open arcade with an elaborately ornamented Sullivanesque frieze incorporating relief sculpture by Richard Bock. This capital is from the second floor of the Heller residence and also demonstrates Sullivan's influence on Wright, here specifically seen in ornament interpreted from Adler & Sullivan's Guaranty Building in Buffalo of 1894–1895. Wright had worked for Adler & Sullivan from 1887 to 1893, at which time he set up his own independent practice. His work up to 1900 is characterized by elements strongly reminiscent of Sullivan's ornament.

PRESERVATION NOTE

Much of the exterior plaster ornament from this house was removed during restoration and replaced with copies made in a more durable material.

Exterior of the Isidore H. Heller house, Chicago, Illinois, 1897.

Capital

Molded plaster, painted
Designed for the Isidore H. Heller house, Chicago, Illinois
c. 1897
Each half: 15⅞ x 20¼ x 9⅝ inches (40.3 x 52 x 24.5 cm)
1988.03.01a,b

AMERICAN LUXFER PRISM COMPANY

Chicago, Illinois, 1897

In 1894, Wright entered a design competition for a projected office building in Chicago for the Luxfer Prism Company. Wright's design incorporated the company's glass blocks in place of the plate-glass windows typically used in commercial buildings. This building that was designed by Wright but not constructed, made greater use of glass within its structural grid than had previous buildings, thus emphasizing the geometry of the skeleton frame. In October 1897, Wright patented a series of designs for glass blocks commissioned by Luxfer, a contract that enabled Wright to add a studio to his Oak Park house. The geometric Luxfer prism designs incorporate a stylized flower of circles and squares. The fluid lines of the flower reflect Sullivan's influence as well as the principles of the English designers Christopher Dresser and Owen Jones and the nineteenth-century French architect Eugène Viollet-le-Duc, each of whom advocated the stylized rendering of botanical forms. For his Luxfer designs, the young architect adapted essentially English ideas, using them as a point of departure for his own solutions to design.

PRESERVATION NOTE

Because the mass-produced Luxfer prisms were incorporated into many undistinguished buildings having nothing to do with Wright, many examples have survived. Collecting Luxfer prisms does not present a preservation problem and over 300 glass blocks, many still within their original sash frames, are in the collection.

Drawing of the projected American Luxfer Prism Company Building, Chicago, Illinois, designed in 1897 but unexecuted.

Three Luxfer prisms

Molded glass
Designed for the American Luxfer Prism Company, Chicago, Illinois
Patented October 4, 1897
Each block: 4 x 4 inches (10 x 10 cm)
1986.42.01

JOSEPH W. HUSSER HOUSE

Chicago, Illinois, 1899

For Wright, a dining room was, in his words, "always a great artistic opportunity." The Husser dining-room set in the collection, designed four years after Wright's own prototype, exemplifies the rectilinear, uncompromising forms for which Wright is best known and which appear early in his career. The slats on the sides of the table enhance the unity of design between table and chairs, which are similarly treated. However, the severity of the chair's design is subtly modified by the outward curve of the crest rails and stiles. Norris Kelly Smith, in his *Frank Lloyd Wright: A Study in Architectural Content* (1966), has this to say about Frank Lloyd Wright's dining-room furniture:

> As Wright perceived, the occasions of dining and of "living" give rise to quite different modes of family grouping. At no time do the members of a family exhibit a greater oneness of purpose than in sitting down together for a meal. In his early houses Wright consistently treats the occasion almost as if it were liturgical in nature. His severely rectilinear furniture, set squarely within a rectilinear context, makes these dining rooms seem more like stately council chambers than like gathering places for the kind of intimate family life we usually associate with Wright's name. They declare unequivocally that the unity of the group requires submission and conformity on the part of its members.

The transitional Husser house, the last that Wright designed before the emergence of his fully developed Prairie style, demonstrated Sullivan's continuing influence in the ornamental and structural detail of the architecture. It was the first of Wright's centrifugal cross-shaped plans, and the first in which the main living quarters were raised above ground, with the basement at ground level. The bedrooms were on yet a third level and there was no attic. This dining-room table may be the one seen on the plan between a built-in buffet and the bay windows. The projecting dining-room bay, reinforced with buttresses, had a commanding view of Lake Michigan.

PRESERVATION NOTE

Unfortunately, the Husser house was demolished around 1924, and this dining-room ensemble is the only furniture that is known to have survived. Although no one attempted to keep the Willits dining-room table and chairs together as a unit, as it was divided up over the years among several museum and private collections, the owners of the Husser set preserved it intact over two generations. Its acquisition in 1987 by Domino's Pizza assures its continued preservation. In the 1920s, when the set was purchased, there were three dining tables and twenty-four matching chairs.

Exterior of the Joseph W. Husser house, Chicago, Illinois, 1899.

Dining table and eight side chairs

Oak; chairs have leather-covered slip-seats
c. 1899
Designed for the Joseph W. Husser house, Chicago, Illinois
Table: 28 x 54 x 60 inches (71.1 x 137.2 x 152.4 cm)
Each chair: 51 ⅞ x 17 ¼ x 17 ¼ inches (131.8 x 43.8 x 43.8 cm)
1987.13.1–9

B. HARLEY BRADLEY HOUSE

Kankakee, Illinois, 1900

This triptych of leaded glass contributed to the unity and harmony of the interior and exterior architecture. The format of the leading subtly echoes the roof lines of the house itself. The Bradley windows are among Wright's earliest to incorporate stylized floral motifs, and the small pieces of ruby glass from the lower vertical windows form the tips of stylized tulips—reminiscent of the principles of Owen Jones and Eugène Viollet-le-Duc, whose works Wright owned and was familiar with. The floral motif extends to the upper sash, or transom, to form a cohesive design. This severely abstract style utilizing formalized motifs is characteristic of Wright's ornament and mature work in art glass. The Bradley house, a dramatic structure showing the influence of Japanese aesthetics, is considered, along with the neighboring Hickox house, among Wright's first Prairie-style houses.

PRESERVATION NOTE

The Bradley house has suffered at the hands of its various owners, who removed both furniture and windows. From 1952 to 1986, the house was used as a restaurant and gift shop. In recent years, furnishings and windows were sold in a series of auctions at Sotheby's and Christie's, the most recent being in December 1987. In 1986, the house was purchased by Stephen B. Small for restoration and adaptive use as an inn. John Eifler, the restoration architect, plans to replicate the original furniture and replace the art glass that had been removed. These windows were originally in the first-floor sitting room that had a view of the Kankakee River. Other windows in the same room were removed for no apparent reason other than the thought of profiting at future auction sales.

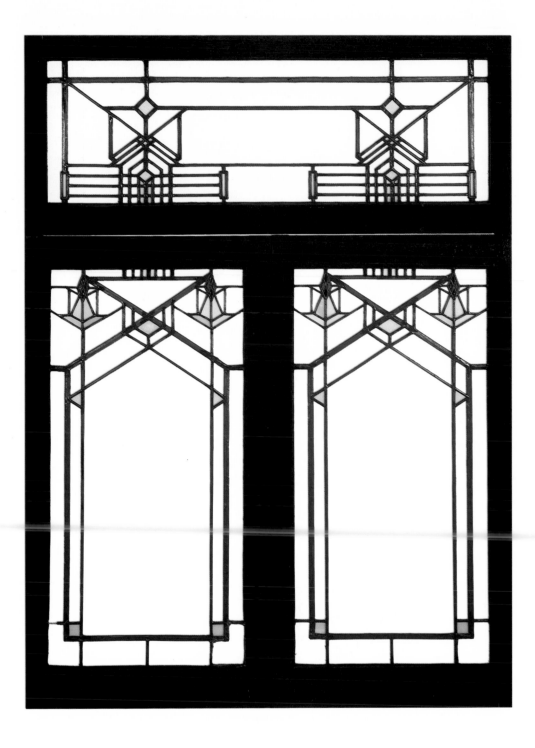

Pair of casement windows and transom

Leaded glass, with original wood frame
Designed for Glenlloyd, the B. Harley Bradley house,
Kankakee, Illinois
c. 1900
Each casement: 41 x 21¾ inches (104 x 55.25 cm)
Transom: 17¾ x 43¼ inches (45.1 x 109.9 cm)
1986.06.01a–c

Wright was in Europe between 1909 and 1911, partly at the invitation of Ernst Wasmuth, to publish this two-volume portfolio of his work. It was the first major publication in Europe of Wright's projects and, therefore, was extremely influential. It has been presumed by Wright scholars that Walter Gropius used one of the plates showing the Mason City bank and offices as the inspiration for his Cologne Werkbund Factory of 1914. A total of 100 images prepared from drawings by Wright, or his assistants, illustrate seventy buildings and projects designed between 1893 and 1909. The plates include perspective views, plans, and sections, as well as interior and exterior details. Wright's introduction appears in German translation and is dated "Florenz, Italien, 15. Mai 1910." An English translation of the introduction, titled "Studies and Executed Buildings," was printed by the Chicago publisher Ralph Fletcher Seymour for inclusion in the sets earmarked for United States distribution.

Exterior of Glenlloyd, the B. Harley Bradley house, Kankakee, Illinois, 1900, illustrated in the catalogue of the Chicago Architectural Club, 1902.

PRESERVATION NOTE

Wright's Wasmuth portfolios were not exempt from destruction any more than were his architectural works. Most of the American editions stored at Taliesin in Spring Green, Wisconsin, were damaged or destroyed in the 1914 fire, and as a result the German editions became better known and more influential in Europe. Unfortunately, contemporary dealers have discovered that these portfolios, intended to stand as a unified presentation, were worth more as individual plates, and thus they have often been broken up and sold individually.

Plate XXII

Living room in Glenlloyd, the B. Harley Bradley house,
Kankakee, Illinois, 1900
Ausgeführte Bauten und Entwürfe von Frank Lloyd Wright/
(Studies and Executed Buildings by Frank Lloyd Wright)
First edition printed in 1910
Brown, grey, gold, white ink on grey and white paper and tissue
72 plates in two portfolios: 28 with tissue overlay,
numbered I through LXIV
26 x 16 inches (60.6 x 40.6 cm)
1986.23.50

WARD WILLITS HOUSE

Highland Park, Illinois, 1902

Wright's remarkable highbacked chairs, of which this is one of the finest examples, are among the earliest of this type of design in the United States. In some respects they are stylistically similar to European designs of the same period, especially when compared with chairs designed by Charles Rennie Mackintosh in 1900 for the Ingram Street Tearooms, Glasgow, Scotland. Architectural periodicals, such as the *London Studio*, contributed to the exchange of artistic ideas between the United States and Europe at the turn of the century, and inspiration was derived from both sides of the Atlantic. Wright, of course, would have known the work of Mackintosh as early as 1899 through American journals such as *The House Beautiful* and also through those published in England. Despite the similarities, the basic governing aesthetic of the two designers was different. Wright consistently employed natural-finish, quarter-inch white oak surfaces in contrast to Mackintosh's later work of painted furniture with ornamental inlay that emphasized the flatness of the design.

Wright used the highbacked dining chair in many of his Prairie interiors such as the Willits house, a Prairie School masterpiece. He first employed this type of chair around 1895 in his own Oak Park house in order to establish and define the space around the dining table and to create a more intimate area; the Willits chair was used this same way.

PRESERVATION NOTE

The second owner of the Willits house removed much of the remaining furniture in the 1950s and sold it at auction. This dining chair is one of two purchased at that time by Mr. and Mrs. Cameron Brown. In 1986, Mrs. Brown consigned this example to Christie's, where it was sold on December 12. Earlier, however, several museums, including The Metropolitan Museum of Art, the High Museum of Art in Atlanta, Georgia, and The St. Louis Art Museum in Missouri, purchased other dining chairs formerly in the Willits house. As it is now, the Willits house is admirably restored for its current owner, incorporating reproductions of some of the original Prairie-style furniture. The National Center for the Study of Frank Lloyd Wright made this dining chair available to John Eifler, the Willits restoration architect, for measured drawings with which to make accurate reproductions. Through the efforts of Sara-Ann Briggs at Domino's Farms, the original Wright drawing for the dining table in the Art and Architecture Library at the University of Michigan was discovered and also made available for the restoration.

The dining room in the Ward Willits house, Highland Park, Illinois, 1902.

Side chair

Oak, with leather-covered slip-seat
Designed for the Ward Willits house, Highland Park, Illinois
c. 1902
55¾ x 17 x 18 inches (141.5 x 43.3 x 45.8 cm)
1986.34.10

ARTHUR HEURTLEY HOUSE

Oak Park, Illinois, 1902

Like most of Wright's furniture, the form of this reclining armchair harmonizes with the architecture of the house for which it was designed. Constructed of Roman brick, the Heurtley house is square in plan with living quarters above ground level. The angularity of this chair, apparent in the termination of the outwardly tapering arms and front legs, corresponds to the projecting prow-like window bays in one of the bedrooms and in the dining room, as well as the angled configurations in the living room, where the chair was originally placed. Birch is an unusual choice of wood for Wright's furniture, as he most often favored the strong grain of oak, corresponding to the interior woodwork. In the same year Wright designed a similar reclining armchair for the Little house in which he repeated the angularity of the front legs and tapering arms as seen in this example.

PRESERVATION NOTE

The original Heurtley furniture was removed from the house when the family moved earlier in the century. At present, none of the original furniture is in the house, whose interior, as with most of Wright's Prairie houses, has been adapted for contemporary living and, in this instance, has been remodeled into apartments. This chair is one of a pair that descended in family ownership until sold at Christie's on December 13, 1985, when it was purchased by the Hirschl & Adler Galleries, New York City. As with so much of Wright's early furniture, this chair was lightened to suit contemporary taste by stripping its original dark finish, which would have harmonized with the interior for which it was designed. Since its acquisition by Domino's Pizza, the original finish has been restored.

Interior of the Arthur Heurtley house, Oak Park, Illinois, 1902.

Reclining armchair

Birch, elm, with leather cushions
Designed for the Arthur Heurtley house, Oak Park, Illinois
c. 1902
37 x 32⅜ x 29½ inches (94 x 82.2 x 74.9 cm)
1986.01.01

SUSAN LAWRENCE DANA HOUSE

Springfield, Illinois, 1902

In his *Ausgeführte Bauten und Enwürfe*, Wright described the Dana house as "a home designed to accommodate the art collection of its owner and for entertaining extensively, somewhat elaborately worked out in detail." The detail that Wright had in mind contributed to the decorative scheme of the house uniting exterior and interior architecture. Formerly part of the exterior ornamental frieze for the Dana house, this fragment incorporates a highly stylized sumac motif, which, according to Wright, "characterizes the expression of one building." Wright was able to create a unified effect by repeating this native Illinois plant in the leaded-glass windows. In the dining room the sumac is used naturalistically in the mural painted by George Niedecken and thus provides a foil for the more general abstracted use. Originally painted green, this section of frieze retains subsequent layers of paint.

Plate XXXIa: exterior of the Susan Lawrence Dana house, Springfield, Illinois, 1902. *Ausgeführte Bauten*.

PRESERVATION NOTE

Because of the deteriorating state of the frieze, it was removed from the house in 1979 before restoration, and replaced with vinyl-coated plywood. In the current restoration, the original frieze will be recast in a more durable material and put back in place. A few sections of the original frieze are now in several museums and private collections.

In 1928, Susan Lawrence Dana moved out of the house, and in 1943, this Wright masterpiece was almost destroyed because of its deteriorating condition through neglect. Soon after, the Charles C. Thomas Publishing Company purchased the house and occupied it until 1981, when it was again threatened with demolition. In that year the state of Illinois purchased the Dana house and after extensive restoration it is now open as a house museum.

Fragment of frieze

Painted plaster
Designed for the Susan Lawrence Dana house, Springfield, Illinois
c. 1902
28 ¼ x 28 inches (71.8 x 71.1 cm)
1986.36.01

Urn

Sheet copper
Designed 1895–1900, this example used in the Susan Lawrence
Dana house, Springfield, Illinois
c. 1902
19 x 19 x 19 inches (48.2 x 48.2 x 48.2 cm)
1985.04.01

Wright's sense of geometric design is evident in this hammered-copper urn that was conceived in conjunction with the vase or weed holder. Both the urn and the vase appear in two drawings in the Archives of The Frank Lloyd Wright Foundation and probably date from the late 1890s. Like the vase, the urn would appear to have been made by James A. Miller, the Chicago sheet-metal worker; one shown in the 1902 exhibition of the Chicago Architectural Club was listed in the catalogue as "*Répoussée* copper bowl. Made by James A. Miller." Wright used the urn in several interiors, including the Avery Coonley house and his own home and studio. Although Sullivan's influence is apparent in the intricate nature of this urn, Wright also strongly asserts his independence in its basic geometric design based on the circle and square that are repeated on all four sides. Originally used in the Susan Lawrence Dana house, this urn was one of two seen in interior photographs and drawings of this house.

PRESERVATION NOTE

This urn was sold at auction in 1943. It remained in private ownership in Springfield until consigned by the daughter of the original purchaser to Christie's, where it was sold on December 13, 1985. Of the several urns known today, none remains in the original architectural setting for which it was designed. To aid the Dana-Thomas Foundation in the effort to acquire as many of the original furnishings as possible, Domino's Pizza will lend this urn to the Dana-Thomas house.

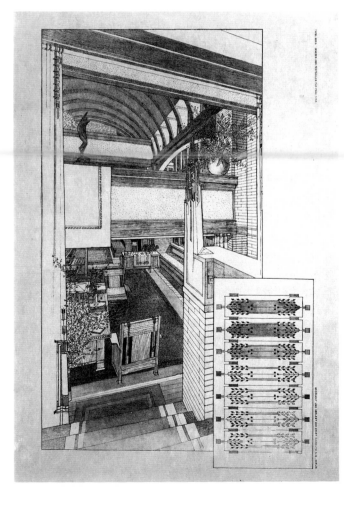

Plate XXXIb: interior of the Susan Lawrence Dana house, Springfield, Illinois, 1902. *Ausgeführte Bauten*.

FRANCIS W. LITTLE HOUSE

Peoria, Illinois, 1903

A forerunner of the hexagonal "barrel" chair that Wright had used in the living room of the Little house in Peoria appeared earlier in the living room of the B. Harley Bradley house in Kankakee, Illinois. The Bradley version has solid-paneled sides and a simplified molding. An almost identical chair with paneled sides in the gallery alcove of the Dana house has supporting legs at each point of the hexagon, while the Little chair has only four legs. The Little residence, a T-plan brick house with a large separate stable, was enlarged by Wright for the second owner, Robert C. Clarke, in 1909. By this date, plans for a second Little house in Wayzata, Minnesota, had begun, but were not executed until 1912 because of Wright's absence in Europe.

PRESERVATION NOTE

Although the Littles took some of the Peoria furniture to their Wayzata house, a small amount was left in Peoria, where it was stored in the basement until sold by Christie's in December 1986 and 1987. One can perhaps fault the owner of the house, Christie's, and even the purchaser for the dispersement of these furnishings from the setting for which they were designed around 1903, but it must be kept in mind that the furniture was stored and had not been used in later transformations of the interior. If the house is not destined to become a museum, as seems unlikely, then the preservation of the furniture in a museum context is a desirable solution. On the other hand, the transfer of furniture from this as well as other houses to private hands could mean that it might not be accessible for future study.

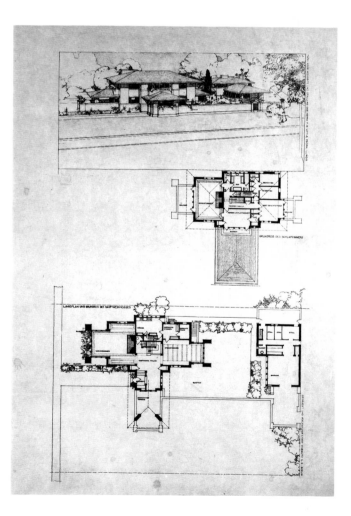

Plate XXVIII: exterior and plan of the Francis W. Little house, Peoria, Illinois, 1903. *Ausgeführte Bauten.*

Armchair

Oak, upholstered seat cushion
Designed for the Francis W. Little house, Peoria, Illinois
c. 1903
23 x 26¾ x 25 inches (58.4 x 68 x 63.5 cm)
1987.10.06

Chest of drawers

Oak, brass pulls
Designed for the Francis W. Little house, Peoria, Illinois
c. 1903
70⅛ x 22⅞ x 27⅞ inches (178 x 57.5 x 70.8 cm)
1987.10.03

Although Wright often designed free-standing furniture, he preferred built-in furniture integral to the architecture. This chest and its identical companion, also now in the Domino's Pizza Collection, has characteristics of both. Although meant to stand alone, the strong rectilinear design gives the chest the appearance of an architectural element within a room. As with most of the furnishings from the Little house, this chest is related to the Dana house furniture, as seen, for instance, in the delicate, rib-like molding on each of the four sides, which parallel a piece in the Dana house. In its original position this chest and its companion flanked the fireplace in the master bedroom, which is shown on Wright's surviving blueprint plan, now privately owned.

PRESERVATION NOTE

In many of Wright's houses, the furnishings were often changed or removed soon after the house was built. That any original furniture remains in a Prairie interior is remarkable. The acquisition of both chests of drawers from the Little master bedroom and the surviving blueprint plan of the room helps us to visualize the space as it was first intended and of which no archival photographs are known at this time.

Side chair

Oak, with original leather-covered slip-seat
Designed for the Francis W. Little house, Peoria, Illinois
c. 1903
39 x 16 x 18½ inches (99.1 x 40.6 x 47 cm)
1986.23.40

This slant-back chair was probably initially designed for this commission, and used subsequently for both the Hillside Home School and the Larkin Administration Building. These chairs were also used in Wright's own Oak Park residence, so he favored them for his personal use as well as for several other commissions. The perforation in the back seen here was not incorporated into the other versions of this chair form, which are slightly varied.

Wall sconce

Brass-plated bronze, opalescent glass
Designed for the Francis W. Little house, Peoria, Illinois
c. 1903
13 ½ x 5 x 4¾ inches (34.3 x 12.7 x 12.1 cm)
1986.23.48

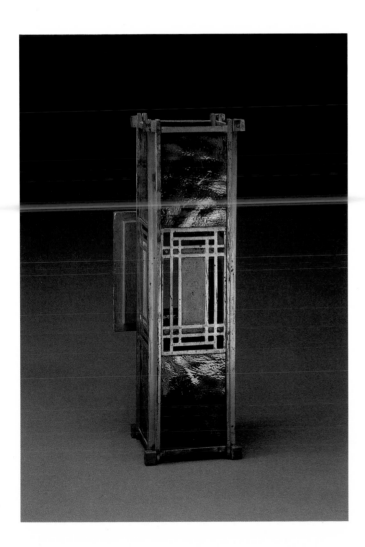

This sconce, with its strongly rectilinear format, was used throughout both the Little and Dana houses, for Wright often used identical or similar forms in commissions of approximately the same date. As may be seen in the Dana house, this particular sconce appeared in three variations. The subdued color of the slightly iridescent amber and green glass and the darkened patina of the metal made the sconce compatible with the Prairie-style palette of earth colors that Wright favored.

PRESERVATION NOTE

When the Littles moved from their Peoria house around 1908, they took a few sconces with them, including this one, but probably never installed them in the Wayzata house. During the dismantling of the Wayzata house in 1972, this sconce was acquired by Donald and Virginia Lovness, who were instrumental in salvaging the interiors later acquired by The Metropolitan Museum of Art. The many artifacts and drawings that survive from this house are due to the initial preservation efforts made by Mr. and Mrs. Lovness.

HILLSIDE HOME SCHOOL

Spring Green, Wisconsin, 1902

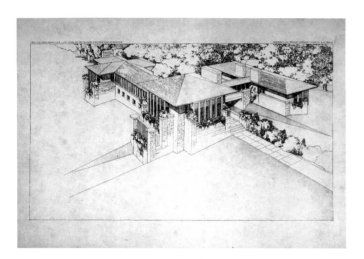

Plate X: exterior of the Hillside Home School, Spring Green, Wisconsin, 1903. *Ausgeführte Bauten*.

The chairs used in the Hillside Home School were also used by Wright with slight variation for the Larkin Administration Building in Buffalo, which was designed in 1904. As with other early Wright furnishings, this chair is characterized by simple, geometric forms, devoid of applied ornament. A solid, canted board runs vertically through the design, extending from the rear stretcher to above the crest rail. This element serves not only as the back rest, but provides added strength to a chair that needed to withstand rigorous use. Wright's chair can be considered both a descendant from, and an antecedent to, certain key European designs. For example, it can be compared to an earlier chair of around 1885 by the English designer E. W. Godwin and to a design of around 1918 by Gerrit Rietveld of Holland. All three have simple frames supporting angled back rests. The Anglo-Japanesque Godwin chair is rectilinear with light, delicate lines and stiles extending well above the crest rail; its upholstered seat and back and turned legs, however, place it in a nineteenth-century context. Likewise, Rietveld's sparse, rectilinear design is comparable to that of Wright's, yet its cantilevered arms and primary colors reflect the influence of the De Stijl movement and modernism. Despite the similarities, Wright's chair is his own. The use of natural fumed oak and corresponding brown leather harmonized with the colors of the Hillside Home School interior.

PRESERVATION NOTE

The original Hillside Home School, a Wright design of 1887, was demolished in 1956. The second school was built around 1903 for Wright's aunts and these chairs were used at that time. In 1933, the school became a part of the Taliesin Fellowship formed in that year. The chairs from the Hillside School have appeared at Christie's in the last few years. Wright favored this design, keeping examples for his own Oak Park house and studio. In 1947, he gave one of the chairs to the design department of The Museum of Modern Art in New York City.

Hillside Home School descended in the family of Wright's sister and was part of the property inherited by the architect. In 1904, Wright designed the assembly and classrooms. In the 1920s, the school closed and the chairs were probably sold at that time. The building stood empty until the 1930s, and the Taliesin Fellowship was formed when Wright added a drafting room, dining room, and theater to the 1903 building. Today, the school is an important part of the Taliesin East complex. The two chairs in the Domino's Pizza Collection descended in the family of Jane Porter, Wright's sister, and were sold at Christie's on May 24, 1984.

Side chair

Oak, with original leather-covered slip-seat
From the Hillside Home School, Spring Green, Wisconsin
c. 1904
39¼ x 15 x 19¼ inches (99.6 x 38 x 48.9 cm)
1986.34.05

LARKIN COMPANY BUILDING

Buffalo, New York, 1904

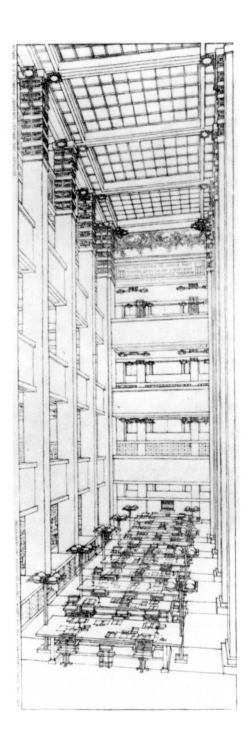

This chair was designed for the brick-and-concrete structure that served as the administrative offices of the Larkin Company's large mail-order house for soap products. The design of the building and furnishings was based on utilitarian considerations, including a concern for offices that would be fireproof. The metal of the furniture echoes the solid geometric severity of the exterior and in contrast to the interior with its light, well-ventilated, and flexible "open" office areas. In *An Autobiography* (1932), Wright described the Larkin furniture: "All the furniture was made in steel and built into place . . . And I made many new inventions . . . All were intended to simplify cleaning and make operation easy." The Larkin furniture invites comparisons with European work of about the same period. This particular chair has a pedestal support similar to Austrian designs by H. Stubner that were published in a 1902 issue of *Das Interieur*. Both designs use a cruciform base with casters but, unlike the Austrian example, Wright's chair has a vertical supporting element. With its swivel seat, Wright's chair was designed for comfort and featured a tilting and perforated back.

PRESERVATION NOTE

According to the architectural historian Jack Quinan, the Larkin Building was in serious financial trouble by 1939 and in 1943 a contractor purchased it for a tax loss. In 1945, the city of Buffalo took it over in a tax foreclosure. According to a newspaper account, "everything removable had been stripped by vandals . . ." Demolition of the building, which began in 1950, represents a major loss among Wright's most important buildings.

Although some of the Larkin furniture survived the demolition, surprisingly little has been preserved in museums or private collections. These few furnishings are the only elements of the original interior design to survive and they convey a sense of the original scale, color, and materials of this outstanding building. Seen individually, and often with deteriorating paint surfaces, this furniture seems out of context, and the role it once played in this dynamic architectural scheme is largely forgotten.

Plate XXXIII: ground plan and exterior of the Larkin Company Building, Buffalo, New York, 1904. *Ausgeführte Bauten.*

Armchair

Painted steel with original leather-covered seat, casters
Designed for the Larkin Company Building,
Buffalo, New York
c. 1904
38 x 24½ x 21 inches (96.5 x 61.6 x 53.3 cm)
1988.02.01

DARWIN D. MARTIN HOUSE

Buffalo, New York, 1904

Although highly stylized, Wright's ornamental vocabulary derives from nature. The repetitive scheme of flowers and leaves as seen in this window, often referred to as the "Tree of Life" pattern, forms the basis of a complex design of clear, opaque, opalescent, and gilt glass. This window was part of a scheme of elaborate art glass employed in the reception area and in the upstairs rooms of the Martin house; *in situ* the window was part of a wall-screen, filtering and transforming the sunlight. Interestingly, the composition relates to the ornamental relief of the same date, designed by Wright and made by Richard W. Bock, for the Larkin Company Building; Darwin D. Martin was the company's secretary. The windows in the Martin house were manufactured by the Linden Glass Company, Chicago.

PRESERVATION NOTE

Removed from the Martin house before it was acquired in 1967 by the State University of New York, Buffalo, this window design is superb as an independent object. However, it is best appreciated in the context of its original architectural setting. The Martin house complex has undergone substantial change. After Mrs. Martin moved out in 1953, the house was left vacant for seventeen years, and was subject to vandalism and deterioration. In 1967, the State University of New York at Buffalo purchased the main house for use as a residence by the university's president. After 1970, the house was used for offices until, in 1982, it was turned over to the university's School of Architecture and Environmental Design, which plans to restore the house.

Plate XXXII: ground plan of the Darwin D. Martin house, Buffalo, New York, 1904. *Ausgeführte Bauten.*

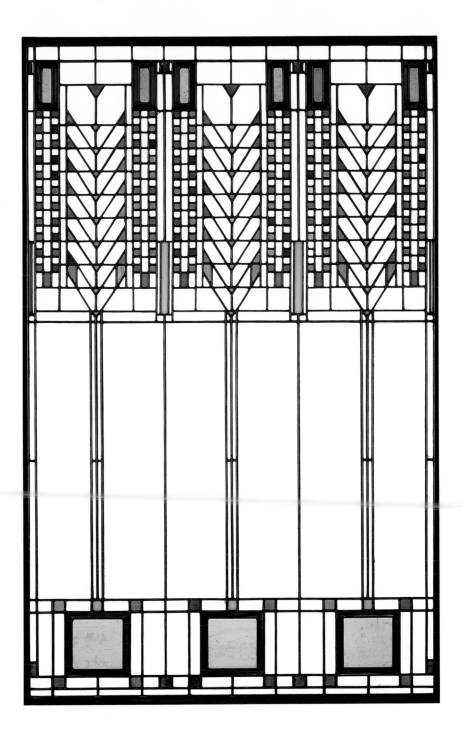

Window, "Tree of Life"

Leaded glass
Designed for the Darwin D. Martin house, Buffalo, New York
c. 1904
39¾ x 27 inches (100.9 x 68.6 cm)
1986.31.01

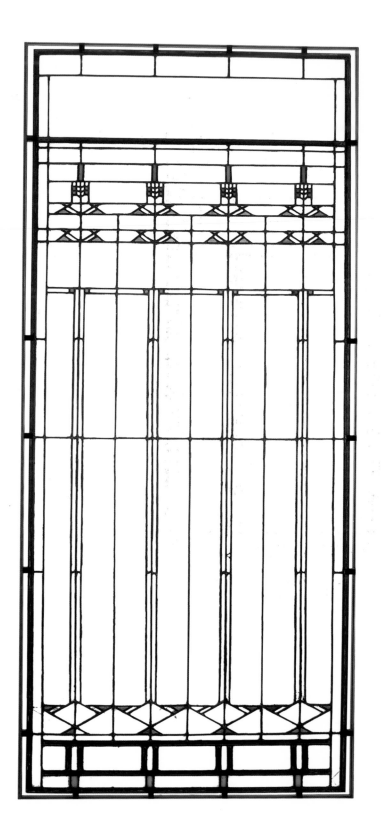

Window

Leaded glass
Designed for the Darwin D. Martin house, Buffalo, New York
c. 1904
58⅜ x 24¼ inches (148.9 x 61.6 cm) (without reproduction frame)
1986.06.10

The Martin house, Wright's largest residential commission at the time, consisted of a house, long gallery, conservatory, and a gardener's cottage. This door was designed for the conservatory that linked the Martin house with the smaller house designed for Martin's sister, Delta Barton. The solid-brass leading was specified to harmonize with the greens and golds of the color scheme. With hundreds of small squares and triangles, the Martin windows created a jewel-like effect.

PRESERVATION NOTE

In 1960, the Martin pergola, conservatory, barn, and greenhouse were demolished to allow space for three new apartment buildings. Although many windows were destroyed at that time, some were sold to museums and private collectors.

Interior of the Darwin D. Martin house conservatory, Buffalo, New York, 1904.

Window

Leaded glass, with original frame
Designed for the Darwin D. Martin house, Buffalo, New York
c. 1904
24½ x 14⅛ inches (62.2 x 35.8 cm)
1986.20.01

The design of this window is related to the Martin house "Tree of Life" window in its employment of a vertical chevron pattern—the stylization of a floral motif—along the right edge. It also relates to designs for the Dana house windows. In both this Martin house window and the Dana house windows, the chevron patterns at the edges are inverted, whereas in the "Tree of Life" window they appear to grow naturally. The Martin house windows as a whole were extremely varied and complex.

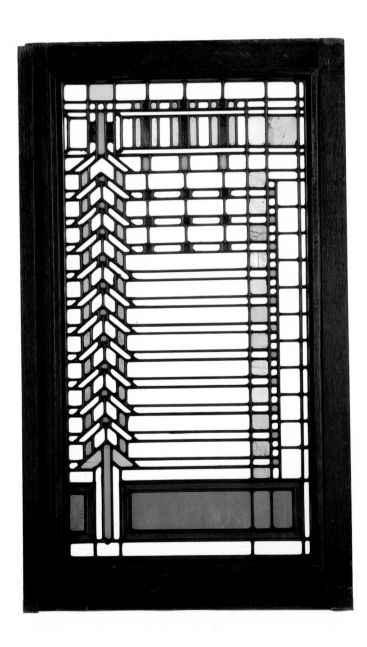

Window

Leaded glass
Designed for the Darwin D. Martin house, Buffalo, New York
c. 1904
22¾ x 32⅛ inches (57.8 x 81.7 cm) (without reproduction frame)
1986.20.02

Eleven windows of this design were installed in the Martin house and nine remain in place. The design of this series takes as its point of departure the windows from the living and dining rooms. Here, however, Wright modified the design by reducing the number of horizontal bands at the top and restricting the vertical ornamentation at either side. In this way Wright successfully turned a vertically oriented design into a horizontal one. As with many of his designs, the organization of the motifs evokes musical rhythm through their repetition and variation and also through their visual similarity to the design of a musical score. Wright himself related his windows to music and the mathematics of its structure.

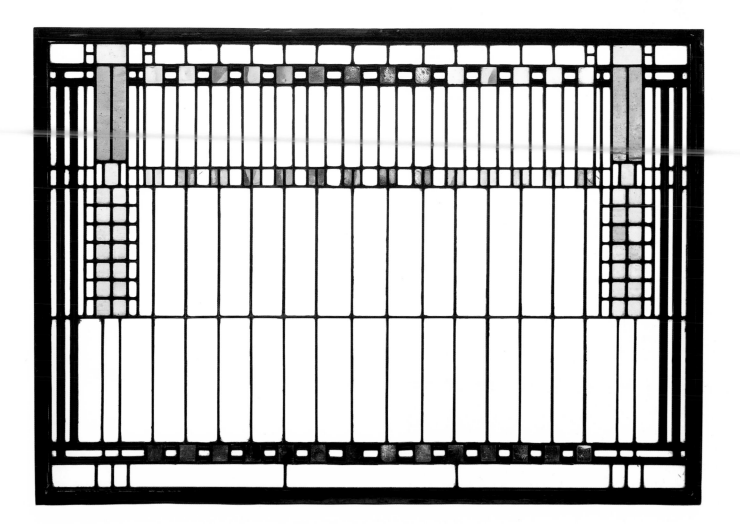

Window

Leaded glass
Designed for the Darwin D. Martin house, Buffalo, New York
c. 1904
38⅝ x 18¾ inches (98.1 x 47.6 cm) (without reproduction frame)
1986.31.02

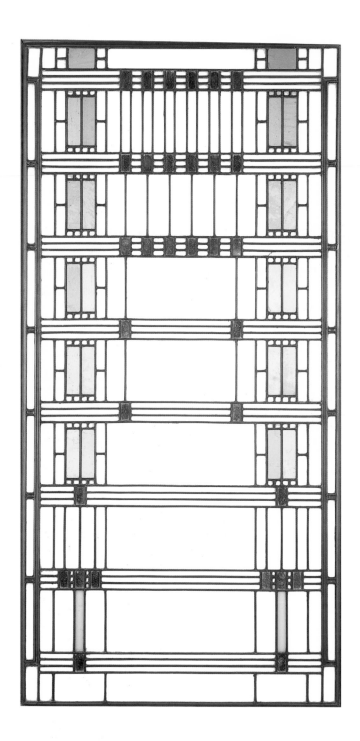

As in the other art-glass windows from the Martin house, this design, although based on natural forms, is also abstract. The symmetrical composition here and in the other windows is typical of Wright's design before he left for Europe in 1909. Here the intricate abstract pattern is concentrated along the edges of the window frame, leaving an unobstructed center. The pattern tends to frame the view.

Living room of the Darwin D. Martin house, Buffalo, New York, 1904.

ISABEL ROBERTS HOUSE

River Forest, Illinois, 1908

This slatted, straight-back chair from the residence of Wright's secretary is a shorter version of the highback chair that Wright initially designed in 1895 for the dining room of his Oak Park residence. A 1908 photograph of the living room of the Avery Coonley house shows a chair very similar to one in the Roberts house. The structural members of this chair are somewhat lighter than are those in the Willits dining chair, marking a transition in Wright's furniture designs, perhaps under the influence of George Niedecken, whose interior-design firm was responsible for carrying out Wright's interiors during this period. The flared front and rear feet, seen also in the dining chairs for the Husser house and later for the Robie house, are typical of Niedecken's Viennese sensibility, which tends to soften Wright's geometry. Although the introduction of these subtle curves relieves the severity of the design, some of the power of the earlier designs is lost. When Wright left for Europe in 1909, abandoning his practice, Niedecken's modifications became more pronounced, weakening the design, as seen in the furnishings of houses that were completed during Wright's absence. Although the Roberts house was two stories in height, it appears from the exterior to have only one level because of the emphasis on the horizontal.

PRESERVATION NOTE

In 1927, this house was resurfaced with brick, and in 1955 the original cruciform-plan house was altered by Wright for Warren Scott. The alterations included replacing the plaster ceiling seen here with blond mahogany. The original furnishings were removed before the Scotts acquired the house.

Living room of the Isabel Roberts house, River Forest, Illinois, 1908.

Side chair

Oak, with leather-covered slip-seat
Designed for the Isabel Roberts house, River Forest, Illinois
c. 1908
39⅜ x 15 x 17⅝ inches (100 x 38 x 44.7 cm)
1986.01.06

RAY W. EVANS HOUSE

Chicago, Illinois, 1908

Designed at the height of Wright's Prairie period, the Evans house, square in plan, was sited on the crest of a low rise in a south Chicago residential area. In this chair, seen *in situ* in the living room, a slight bow to the back is an element that softens Wright's more characteristic geometric and rectilinear designs. This treatment of the back may have provided greater comfort, but the forcefulness and strength of Wright's furniture designs of just a few years earlier have now been compromised to some degree. This tendency toward greater complexity may also be seen in the feet of this chair.

PRESERVATION NOTE

Much of the Evans furniture remained in the house until 1970, when the owner gave three windows, a library table, and three armchairs—including this one—to The Art Institute of Chicago. Unfortunately, the original finish on the furniture, which would have corresponded to the interior woodwork, was painted over. In the refinishing, a lighter stain was used, thus again modifying the effect that Wright had originally intended. In 1985, the Art Institute sold this chair as a duplicate to Scott Elliott, a Chicago dealer, from whom it was acquired by Domino's Pizza. The chair's light finish has now been darkened to represent the original color.

Living room of the Ray W. Evans house, Chicago, Illinois, 1908.

Armchair

Oak
Designed for the Ray W. Evans house, Chicago, Illinois
c. 1908
34¼ x 30¼ x 24 inches (87 x 76.8 x 61 cm)
1986.08.05

AVERY COONLEY HOUSE

Riverside, Illinois, 1908

Following Wright's designs, the interior decorative scheme of the Coonley house was completed after Wright's departure for Europe in 1909. The table is among a small group of Coonley furniture to survive; a smaller table is seen *in situ* in plate LVI of the Wasmuth portfolio, *Ausgefürhte Bauten und Entwürfe*, illustrating the Coonley living room. The interior architect responsible for supervising completion of the Coonley interiors was George Niedecken of the Niedecken-Wallbridge Company in Milwaukee, Wisconsin. Renderings for the Coonley furniture are in the Prairie Archive at the Milwaukee Art Museum.

PRESERVATION NOTE

The furnishings were removed long before a fire destroyed the living room of the Avery Coonley house, which has now been reconstructed. This table was sold at Christie's on December 12, 1986.

Exterior of the Avery Coonley house, Riverside, Illinois, 1908.

Interior of the Avery Coonley house, Riverside, Illinois, 1908.

Library table

Oak
Designed for the Avery Coonley house, Riverside, Illinois
c. 1908
38⅞ x 65¼ x 28¼ inches (98.7 x 165.7 x 71.7 cm)
1987.17.18

Two windows

Leaded glass
Designed for the Avery Coonley house, Riverside, Illinois
c. 1908
Each: 32 x 20⅛ inches (81.2 x 51 cm)
framed together in a reproduction frame
1985.01.05,06

In *An Autobiography*, Wright described his work on the Coonley house, which is considered the culmination of his Prairie period: "I feel now, looking back upon it, that building was the best I could then do in the way of a house." The horizontal lines of the Coonley house were emphasized by the placement of the casement windows. Although each window was vertically oriented, placing them side by side created a strong horizontal band. The asymmetrical arrangement of the leaded design was mirrored in the matching window, exemplifying Wright's idea of continuity. This same concept was developed more elaborately in the windows for the Francis W. Little house of 1913. Designed for one of the service buildings containing the garage, these Coonley windows are the simplest of three types used in the house, illustrated in Plate LVII of *Ausgefürhte Bauten und Entwürfe*.

PRESERVATION NOTE

These two windows were removed to allow for alterations in construction. They are part of a group of four identical designs, with slight variations in size, in the Domino's Pizza Collection.

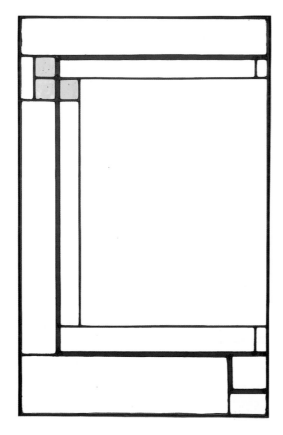 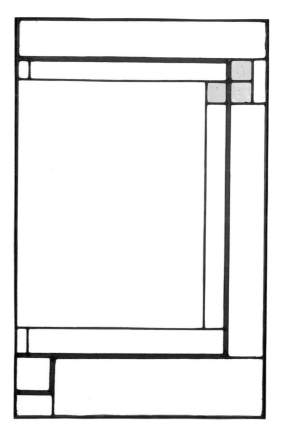

Two windows

Leaded glass
Designed for the Avery Coonley house, Riverside, Illinois
c. 1908
Each: 29⅜ x 14 inches (74.7 x 35.5 cm)
For two in reproduction frames: 35 x 37¼ inches (88.9 x 94.6 cm)
1986.20.04a,b

These windows, which stress verticality by isolating the abstract pattern from the clear glass, were designed for the dining room of the Coonley house, where they are seen with the dining table and chairs designed by the English architect M. H. Baillie Scott. The sense of geometry that they convey was carried through the entire architectural scheme, exterior as well as interior. The windows relate to the polychrome tiles used on the exterior facade and also to the exterior lighting fixtures. Inside, Wright used variations of these squares and rectangles in the patterns on the rugs and on some of the upholstery. This particular window design and two others were illustrated in *Ausgefürhte Bauten und Entwürfe*.

PRESERVATION NOTE

The Coonley house has suffered many indignities over the years and, in 1969, suffered further by being divided into three separate apartments. Although the Coonley family left the original furnishings intact, subsequent owners sometimes acted with less concern for the integrity of the architecture and disposed of most of this furniture as well as some of the windows. Further damage occurred in June 1977, when a disastrous fire destroyed the main living room and severely damaged the original bedroom wing.

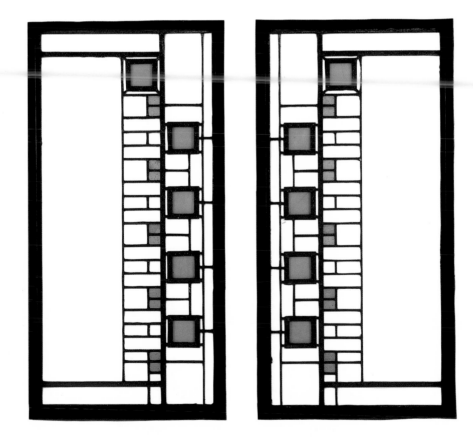

Sconce

Bronze, frosted glass globe, mica
Designed for the Avery Coonley house, Riverside, Illinois
c. 1908
7¼ x 11 x 9 inches (18.4 x 28 x 22.8 cm)
1986.20.06

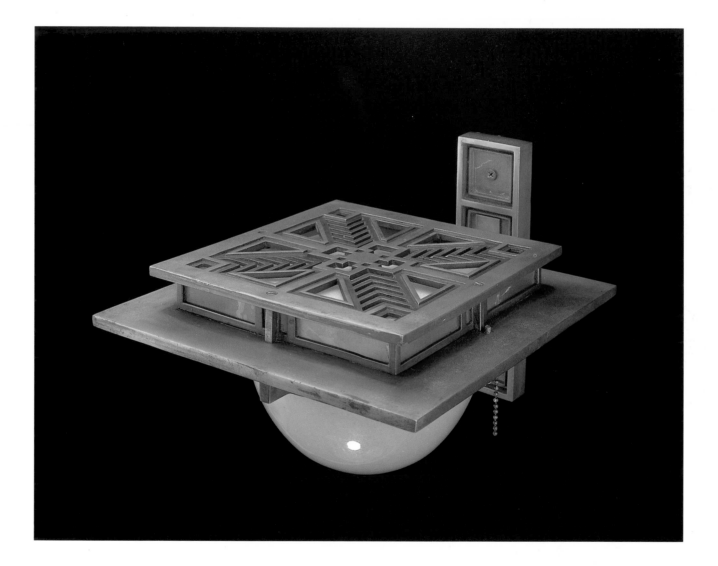

Lighting was always an important part of Wright's architectural schemes. He employed a variety of sources including natural light, which filtered through windows and skylights, and artificial light provided by hanging fixtures, desk and table lamps, and wall sconces. This sconce, used throughout much of the interior of the Coonley house, including the dining room, has a geometric perforated cover plate whose pattern is visible from either below or above. The pattern is based on an abstraction of fern leaves, the motif also used in the living room ceiling grilles; the fern motif is also naturalistically rendered in a fireplace mural painted by the Chicago interior designer George Niedecken. The deep golden tonality of the bronze and the dark hue of the fumed oak wall plate are typical of Wright's palette. Wright used the sconce in other projects of the same date, for example in the Frederick Robie and Meyer May houses. A drawing in the Archives of The Frank Lloyd Wright Foundation shows three varieties of wall sconces called "electric fixture[s]" to be used at the Coonley house.

PRESERVATION NOTE

Removing lighting fixtures from Wright houses is as serious an error as removing windows, since they are difficult to replace and integral to the architecture. Changes made to the Coonley house when it was converted into multiple dwellings probably necessitated such alterations.

Dining room of the Avery Coonley house, Riverside, Illinois, 1907.

THE ART INSTITUTE OF CHICAGO

Chicago, Illinois, 1908

In 1905, accompanied by his first wife, Catherine, and his clients, Mr. and Mrs. Ward Willits, Wright made his first visit to Japan, where his interest in Japanese art and culture grew. Upon his return, his fervor for collecting Japanese prints increased and he often recommended their purchase to his clients. In *An Autobiography*, Wright acknowledged the influence of the Japanese print: "During the years at the Oak Park workshop, Japanese prints intrigued me and taught me much. The elimination of the insignificant, a process of simplification in art in which I was engaged, beginning with my twenty-third year, found collateral evidence in the print. . . . Japanese art, I found, really did have organic character, was nearer to the earth and a more indigenous product of native conditions of life and work, therefore more nearly modern as I saw it, than European civilization alive or dead." This print-stand form, designed for display, was, in a larger version, used in the living room of Taliesin East; this stand may be the one included in the exhibition of Wright's own collection of Japanese prints at The Art Institute of Chicago in 1908. The print stand is typical of Wright's Prairie style in its rectilinearity, the dark stain, and the vertical slats similar in style to his dining-room chairs of a few years earlier.

PRESERVATION NOTE

It is not known for which house this print stand was originally intended. A specific provenance, however, is often the key element in documenting Wright's designs and thus assuring their authenticity.

Japanese Print Show, The Art Institute of Chicago,
Chicago, Illinois, 1908.

Print stand

Mahogany, Japanese print (not original to stand)
c. 1908
35 ½ x 8 ⅝ x 10 ⅝ inches (90 x 22 x 27 cm)
1986.08.13

Exterior of the Avery Coonley Playhouse, Riverside, Illinois, 1912.

AVERY COONLEY PLAYHOUSE

Riverside, Illinois, 1912

On his return from Europe, Wright received a second important commission from Avery Coonley, this time for a small building to serve as a kindergarten, or playhouse, so-called because it contained a stage. The kindergarten was actually a "progressive" school for the Coonley children and for other children as well; it was one of several organized in Riverside by Mrs. Coonley.

According to Wright, the two-dimensional abstract designs of the windows for the Coonley Playhouse are based on his observation of a parade with balloons, flags, and confetti, motifs suitable for a kindergarten. These windows—his greatest achievement in art glass—are also among the first non-objective, geometric designs executed by Wright upon his return from Europe, where he must have been influenced by the avant-garde work of such artists as Robert Delaunay and Frantisek Kupka. In their original setting, the clerestory windows formed a continuous design. The abstract, colorful arrangement of circles and squares is restricted to the upper portion in some of the windows. Although each window is unique, they are unified by a single horizontal leading that separates the larger top section from the bottom. These horizontal clerestory windows are related to the other windows in the Playhouse and form a cohesive composition through the content of their design. Drawings for the Playhouse windows are in the Archives of The Frank Lloyd Wright Foundation.

PRESERVATION NOTE

Because of the architectural alterations to the Playhouse, these critically important windows are preserved as a unit at Domino's Farms. Around 1967, the windows were removed from the Playhouse; most were stored, but a few were sold by the Bud Holland Gallery, Chicago. In 1986, the windows were under consideration by two American art museums as well as by a Japanese private collector. At that time they were bought for the Domino's Pizza Collection.

Window triptych

Leaded glass
Designed for the Avery Coonley Playhouse, Riverside, Illinois
c. 1912
Framed ensemble: 40½ x 64½ inches (102.7 x 165 cm.)
1986.25.01a–c

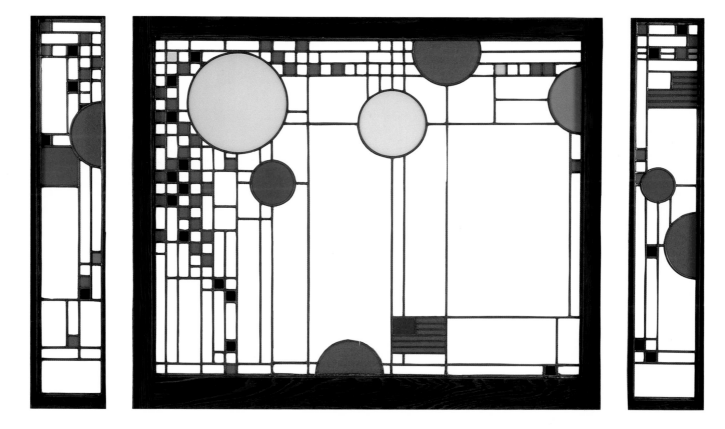

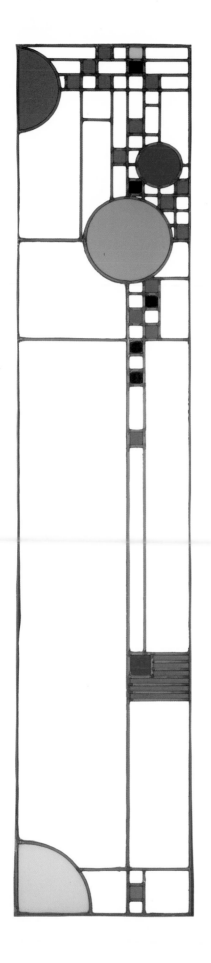

Window

Leaded glass
Designed for the Avery Coonley Playhouse, Riverside, Illinois
c. 1912
60½ x 12½ inches (153.7 x 31.8 cm.)
1986.06.05

Clerestory windows

Leaded glass, with original frames
Designed for the Avery Coonley Playhouse, Riverside, Illinois
c. 1912
86.25.13, 24 x 38⅜ inches (61 x 97.5 cm)
86.25.10, 24 x 38⅜ inches (61 x 97.5 cm)
86.25.20, 24 x 38⅜ inches (61 x 97.5 cm)
86.25.23, 24 x 38⅜ inches (61 x 97.5 cm)
86.25.27, 24 x 38⅜ inches (61 x 97.5 cm)
86.25.22, 24 x 38⅜ inches (61 x 97.5 cm)

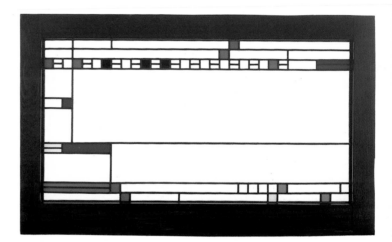

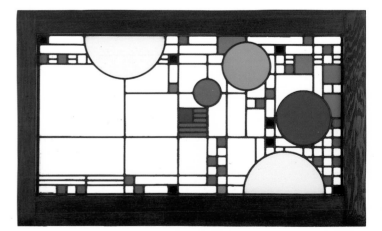

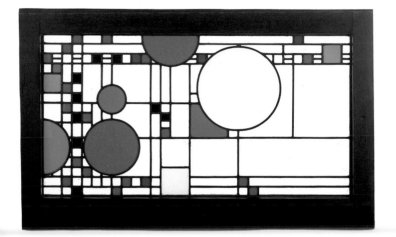

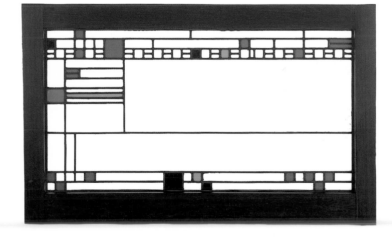

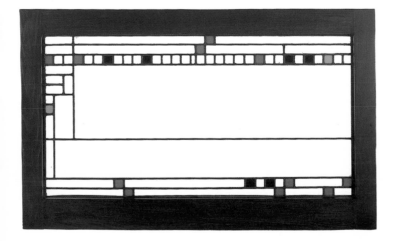

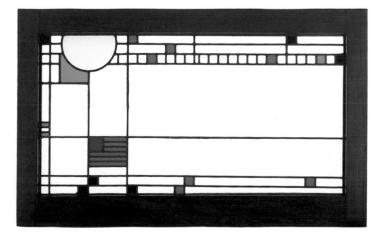

Child's side chair

Birch, with leather-covered slip-seat and back
Designed for the Avery Coonley Playhouse, Riverside, Illinois
c. 1912
31 x 15¼ x 16⅜ inches (78.7 x 38.7 x 41.5 cm)
1985.02.04

This chair, one of four in the collection, was part of a larger group placed around tables whose form combined circular and octagonal elements. The slab-like back of the chairs relates to the earlier Hillside Home School, Little, and Larkin chairs.

PRESERVATION NOTE

Although the Playhouse furniture was left *in situ* after the Coonleys moved to Washington, D.C., in 1917, the chairs were later dispersed and the building itself was significantly altered for single-family use. Today, the Playhouse is being restored by the Chicago architect John Vinci.

Interior of the Avery Coonley Playhouse, Riverside, Illinois, 1912.

WILLIAM B. GREENE HOUSE

Aurora, Illinois, 1912

Furniture from Wright's early career can be related to aesthetic principles promulgated by the American Arts and Crafts Movement, and this settle is comparable to one made by Gustav Stickley that is illustrated in *The Craftsman* for October 1901. Both settles have slatted backs and sides and square-section legs, armrests, and crestrails. While the seat of Wright's settle extends forward, the seat of the Stickley settle does not. Although Wright scorned Mission furniture as "plain as a barn door," it was used in some of the secondary rooms that he designed when his own furniture could not be afforded. The flange-like square-section foot of Wright's settle is seen in English examples from this period by C. F. A. Voysey. Wright's other settles are quite different from this example: those designed in the 1890s and 1900s for the William H. Winslow, Darwin D. Martin, and Frederick Robie houses are made with solid-panel sides and back with attenuated, cantilevered arms. Just as the Robie and Martin settles originally had upholstered cushions on the seat and back, this settle from the Greene house undoubtedly had cushions at the back.

Exterior of the William B. Greene house, Aurora, Illinois, 1912.

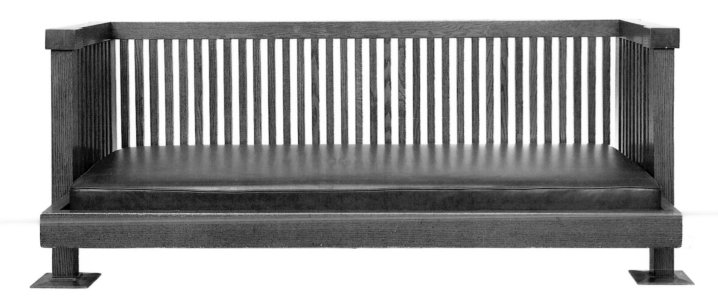

Settle

Oak, with leather-covered seat cushion
Designed for the William B. Greene house, Aurora, Illinois
c. 1912
30½ x 80 x 32¾ inches (77.5 x 203 x 83.3 cm)
1986.18.01

FRANCIS W. LITTLE HOUSE

Wayzata, Minnesota, 1912

In 1908, Francis W. Little joined the Federal Reserve Banking System as a vice president of the Minnesota Trust Company. This move followed his selling of the Wright house in Peoria, Illinois, and led to his commissioning a second house from Wright to be built in Wayzata, a Minneapolis suburb. According to correspondence between Wright and Francis Little, now in the collection of The Metropolitan Museum of Art, the architect made compromises in the design of this second house. Many of the client's objections were centered on the designs for the ornamental glass intended for the principal rooms. Little did not like the rectilinearity and the restraint of Wright's proposed pattern nor did he like the prominent green color. The pair of doors now in the collection are of the nearly colorless glass on which Wright finally settled, but they still reflect the restraint of the first scheme that he had proposed. Together, they form a symmetrical composition, while the design of each is a simplified version of the central panel of windows designed for the Littles' living room, now installed in The Metropolitan Museum of Art.

PRESERVATION NOTE

In 1972, the Little heirs decided to demolish Northome in order to build a more traditional house. The Metropolitan Museum of Art purchased all the interiors as a way of preserving them. In 1981, the living room became a part of the Metropolitan's new American Wing. The library of the Little house was acquired by the art museum in Allentown, Pennsylvania, and was installed in 1978. In 1986, Domino's Pizza purchased the bedroom wing. Thus the Little residence, which was particularly sensitive to the site for which it was designed, has been divided and distributed, but fortunately, these important interiors have been preserved and they succeed in conveying some sense of Wright's intention. The Minneapolis Museum of Art purchased smaller fragments of the house. Unfortunately, none of the museums that purchased rooms and artifacts pursued the option of preserving the entire house *in situ*, as a house museum, and persuading the Little heirs to build elsewhere.

Exterior of Northome, the Francis W. Little house, Wayzata, Minnesota, 1912.

Pair of doors

Leaded glass, with original frame and surround
Designed for Northome, the Francis W. Little house, Wayzata,
Minnesota
c. 1912
78 x 42 x 7¾ inches (198.1 x 106.7 x 19.7 cm)
1986.04.02

MIDWAY GARDENS

Chicago, Illinois, 1914

In late autumn 1913, Edward Waller, Jr., son of one of Wright's earliest clients, approached Wright to create an entertainment center on Cottage Grove Avenue, near the University of Chicago, that would have a variety of spaces both indoors and out for dining, dancing, and listening to music—modeled, in fact, after the outdoor garden restaurants of Germany. Midway Gardens, as it came to be known, provided the architect with an opportunity to design an elaborate architectural complex with a rich decorative scheme of great variety and invention, including all interior furnishings down to such details as porcelain place settings. This oval plate, one of a small group of pieces known to have survived, is simply decorated with a single row of red squares about the rim. It is one of four in the collection, each marked "New York–Chicago/Bauscher/Weiden(Germany)/1914." Two drawings in the Archives of The Frank Lloyd Wright Foundation show a teacup and saucer of the same design in elevation and plan. In *An Autobiography*, Wright wrote that he had based his designs for Midway Gardens, which included murals, sculpture, and accessories, on abstract principles. The designs suggest that Wright had thoroughly assimilated the abstract experiments by the various Secessionist architects and artists whose works he must have seen in Europe in 1909–1910. For instance, the murals for Midway Gardens reflected Frantisek Kupka's constellar works, and the sculpture, executed by Wright's assistants, Alfonso Iannelli and Richard Bock, recalls the work of the Cubists, as well as sculpture designed by Josef Hoffmann. In fact, the decorative squares on the plate were a motif frequently used by Hoffmann and other Viennese Secessionists, and it was one of the elements Wright employed to give his vast complex unity.

PRESERVATION NOTE

Because of declining profits, Midway Gardens was sold in 1916 to The Edelweiss Brewing Company. In 1920, Prohibition brought an end to Midway's operation as a beer garden and it was sold again for use as a garage and carwash. Midway Gardens was finally razed in 1929 and a few architectural elements and ceramics are the only artifacts to survive from a commission where Wright attempted to unite all the arts—music, sculpture, and painting—under his direction. According to *An Autobiography*, Wright himself was unhappy about the alteration to his building and the decorative scheme, and he hoped someone would "give them the final blow and tear them down."

View of the Summer Garden at Midway Gardens, Chicago, Illinois, 1914.

Plate

Glazed porcelain
Designed for Midway Gardens, Chicago, Illinois
c. 1914
6¼ x 9¾ inches (15.8 x 24.8 cm)
1986.03.04

Sprite head

Concrete
Designed for Midway Gardens, Chicago, Illinois
c. 1914
15 x 10½ x 9 inches (38.1 x 26.7 x 22.9 cm)
1987.05.01

Geometric forms and shapes were prevalent in the decorative scheme throughout Midway Gardens. These forms and shapes may derive from Wright's childhood experience with games designed by the German educator Friedrich Froebel to encourage children to understand nature's underlying geometric forms. Froebel blocks were used to create structures approximating the child's environment and thus may have symbolized play in Wright's memory, an appropriate association for a structure whose function was dedicated to amusement. In addition, Wright's trip to Europe, where he saw avant-garde painting and sculpture, may also have provided him with the impetus to use geometric forms for his decorative motifs. The "sprites" in the summer garden, of which this head is an example, were a joint effort by Wright and the sculptors Alfonso Iannelli and Richard Bock. Iannelli made scale drawings and models before they were approved by Wright for final execution in concrete. Their inclusion in the gardens shows Wright's interest in the work of the Cubists in France. The overlapping horizontal and vertical planes, which do not appear in Wright's work prior to his trip to Europe, can be related to Cubist paintings and sculptures. According to Edgar Kaufmann, jr, the Iannelli statues were closely related to those in the Kunstschaus designed by Josef Hoffmann in 1908, which Wright may have seen in publication or perhaps while in Europe.

A sprite sculpture at Midway Gardens, Chicago, Illinois, 1914.

Entrance to Midway Gardens, Chicago, Illinois, 1914.

PRESERVATION NOTE

Examples of these sprite figures survive in several private and museum collections. According to Scott Elliott, this head was acquired from the Iannelli estate and was a studio maquette for the Midway sculptures.

IMPERIAL HOTEL

Tokyo, Japan, 1921

Although Wright began designs for the Imperial Hotel, one of his greatest architectural achievements, in 1915 and construction began two years later, the hotel was not complete until 1922. Wright created a cohesive unity for the hotel and its furnishings: for example, the hexagonal shape of the back of this side chair was also employed in the table tops and reflected the ceiling design of the central lounge. A drawing for these chairs, dated February 15, 1921, is in the Archives of The Frank Lloyd Wright Foundation. Replacements for these fragile chairs were made while the hotel was still operating, and most surviving examples in museum collections, including this one, were made after the 1920s. As seen in archival photographs, the original chairs had caning on the back, seat, and sides, often with attached back cushions. The yellow Naugahyde found on so many of the later production chairs would appear to be a covering that dates just prior to, or after, World War II.

PRESERVATION NOTE

With the demolition of the Imperial Hotel in 1968, one of Wright's major architectural works was lost. The commission is now known through photographs and the furnishings that survive, including this side chair, which is one of several preserved in American museums.

Interior of the Imperial Hotel, Tokyo, Japan, 1916–1922.

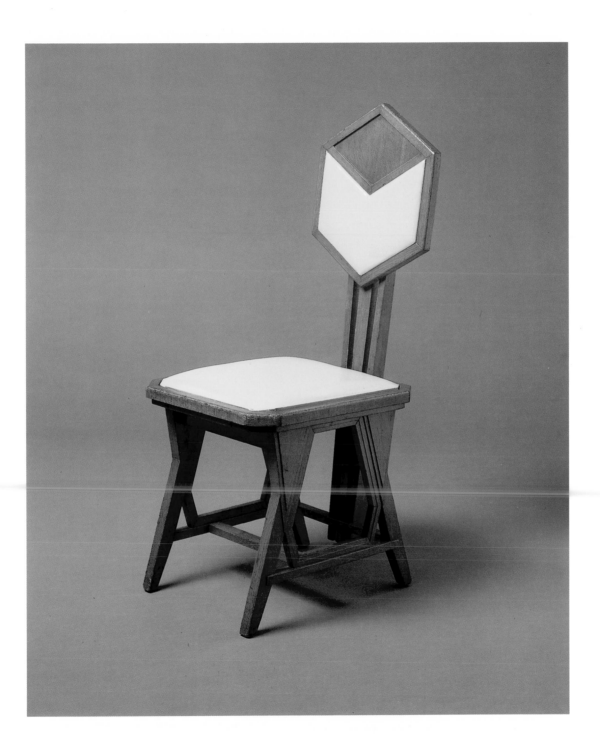

Side chair

Oak, with original oil–cloth slip–seat and back
Designed for the Imperial Hotel, Tokyo, Japan
c. 1921; this example probably made c. 1930
38 x 15¾ x 20 inches (96.5 x 40 x 51 cm)
1986.01.03

Exterior of the Imperial Hotel, Tokyo, Japan, 1916–1922.

Ornamental detail in the Imperial Hotel, Tokyo, Japan,
1916–1922.

Architectural ornament

Terra-cotta
Designed for the Imperial Hotel, Tokyo, Japan
1916–1922
8½ x 8¼ x 2½ inches (21.6 x 21 x 6.3 cm)
1986.23.43

Terra-cotta, as seen in this architectural detail, was used by
Wright on the exterior and interior arcades of the Imperial
Hotel to achieve a rich mosaic-like effect similar to that of the
Midway Gardens and the California houses that he designed in
this same period. Other materials used in the hotel were
copper and a lava-like native stone called *oya*.

PRESERVATION NOTE

Although the Imperial Hotel emerged largely intact from the great
1923 earthquake and did not suffer during World War II, it was
altered by the American military in the early years of the Occupation
of Japan. During the winter of 1967–1968, the hotel was demolished
due to economic considerations. The entrance lobby was dismantled
and reconstructed in 1976 at the Meiji Village, a field museum 230
miles west of Tokyo.

Carpet fragment

Wool
Designed for the Imperial Hotel, Tokyo, Japan
1916–1922
17 x 8¼ inches (43.2 x 21 cm)
1986.23.45

Like Midway Gardens, the Imperial Hotel was a large complex unified by its geometric decorative scheme that included the design of all interior details: furniture, carpets, textiles, silver, and ceramics. While some decorative objects survived the hotel's demolition, most of the elaborate textiles were lost. A piece of upholstery fabric in the collections of The Frank Lloyd Wright Foundation and this carpet fragment are notable exceptions. The overall design of the carpet, which was originally in the main dining room, relates to the hotel's ceramic design and reflects the building's architecture. An impression of the carpet *in situ* can be gained from the black-and-white photographs of the hotel's interior that have been published. Wright described the importance of floor coverings in his buildings: "Floor coverings and hangings are at least as much a part of the house as the plaster on the walls or the tiles on the roof."

PRESERVATION NOTE

In this fragment of carpet one senses an important aspect of Wright's architecture that is often lost: the rich color scheme that helps to emphasize the dramatic interior spaces.

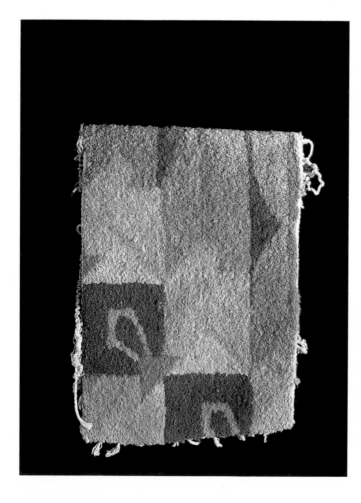

Place setting

Glazed porcelain
Designed for the Imperial Hotel, Tokyo, Japan
1916–1922; this example from 1964–1966
Measurement of plate: 7⅝ inches (19.4 cm)
1987.16.01–6

The design of the china place setting for the Imperial Hotel is very reminiscent of the designs of the Coonley Playhouse windows and the mural at Midway Gardens. In the original place settings, the circular motifs continued into the cup itself, a detail that brings to mind Nabeshima ware, a type of eighteenth-century Japanese porcelain that may have appealed to Wright. The original china was made from fine porcelain that was not suitable for rigorous hotel use. To replace damaged and broken sets, the Imperial ordered more durable china of the same design from the 1920s until the 1960s, but the earlier delicacy and sensitivity were lost.

HOLLYHOCK HOUSE

Hollywood, California, 1920

As in the other decorative elements of Aline Barnsdall's house, details in this exterior lantern abstract the hollyhock and trellis. The lamp includes elements similar to those seen in other interior furnishings, such as the small squares placed on the central vertical axis of the lamp to represent hollyhock buds. The trapezoidal form at the top is repeated at the bottom to preserve symmetry, and its geometric divisions emphasize the balanced composition. By means of some early photographs, three other lanterns of this design have been located: a pair that flanked the entrance to the Garden Court, of which this example is presumably one, and at the kennels, where one of the lanterns remains *in situ*.

PRESERVATION NOTE

According to Frank Lloyd Wright's grandson, Eric, his father, Lloyd Wright, removed furnishings from the house during the 1946–1948 renovation, and these were stored in the chauffeur's quarters in the garage. However, when construction began in 1954 in the Wright-designed gallery that incorporated the garage, the furnishings could not be found. Virginia Kazor, curator of Hollyhock House, says that if the original lantern were to be reinstalled, it might well be stolen. In this instance, therefore, preserving the original lantern in a museum and including a reproduction in the restoration is an acceptable solution.

Exterior of Hollyhock House (Aline Barnsdall house), Los Angeles, California, 1920.

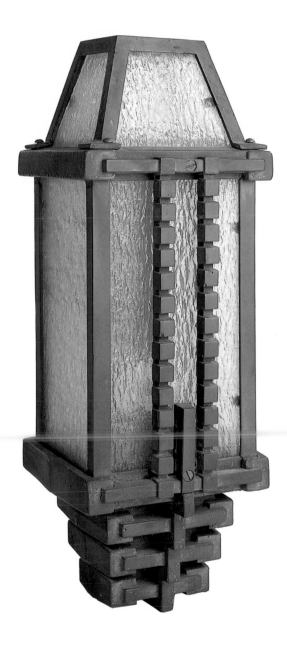

Lantern

Bronze, textured glass
Designed for Hollyhock House (Aline Barnsdall house),
Hollywood, California
c. 1920
19½ x 7 x 7¼ inches (49.5 x 17.8 x 18.5 cm)
1986.08.12

Window

Leaded glass
Designed for Hollyhock House (Aline Barnsdall house),
Hollywood, California
c. 1920
71 ¼ x 6 inches (181 x 15.2 cm)
1986.08.11

Wright worked on the Barnsdall house on his brief trips to the United States while he was building the Imperial Hotel in Tokyo. The window in the collection achieves a unified effect by the repetition of an ornamental motif based on the hollyhock. This stylized motif was also used on the backs of the dining-room chairs, where the flower buds were represented by small squares, while the rectilinear panels acted as a "trellis" for the buds. This pattern is repeated on a smaller scale on the dining-room walls and on the concrete frieze of the exterior.

PRESERVATION NOTE

Given to the city of Los Angeles in 1927, Hollyhock House retains most of its art-glass windows and some of the Wright-designed furniture. This window, originally located in the music room facing the foyer, was replaced by a reproduction during restoration. The house became part of the Los Angeles Municipal Art Museum before its restoration, opening as a house museum in the early 1970s. Inasmuch as the glass used in Hollyhock House is still available, it was possible to make accurate reproductions of missing glass.

Interior of Hollyhock House (Aline Barnsdall house),
Los Angeles, California, 1920, showing the fireplace and skylight.

FALLINGWATER

Mill Run, Pennsylvania, 1936

Fallingwater, the summer house of the Pittsburgh department store owner, Edgar Kaufmann, was Wright's most important domestic commission after the Robie house in Chicago. According to *Architectural Forum* for January 1938, Wright created a "living space over and above the stream upon several terraces upon which a man who loved the place sincerely, one who liked to listen to the waterfall, might well live." Fallingwater, located in a secluded and wooded area some 100 miles south of Pittsburgh, illustrates Wright's principle of designing a house to conform to, and to be shaped by, its site. The top and supports of this table, probably designed for the servants' wing, echo the cantilevered forms of the house itself. The refined craftsmanship by the Gillen Woodworking Company of Milwaukee indicates the quality of the artisans responsible for making the Kaufmann furniture.

PRESERVATION NOTE

In 1963, Edgar Kaufmann, jr, gave Fallingwater to the Western Pennsylvania Conservancy as a museum open to the public. The house retains most of its original furnishings, a combination of Wright-designed pieces and European and American antiques. According to Lynda S. Waggoner, curator and administrator of Fallingwater: "This design was never replaced by another, and how the table left Fallingwater remains unclear. The daughter of a former Kaufmann family servant contends that the table was given by Edgar Kaufmann, Sr., to her father. Edgar Kaufmann, jr, has emphatically stated that such an occurrence would have been highly unlikely. . . . Lastly, concerning our wishes regarding whether or not the table should be returned to Fallingwater: to the best of my knowledge, only two examples of the original furnishings were ever removed from the site. Both were side tables: the tall table now in the Domino's collection, and a shorter version of the same table which was sold a few years ago. Although it would be wonderful to claim that all of our furnishings remain intact, we do not feel uncomfortable with this table remaining in the Domino's collection, where it may be studied in the greater context of Wright's other decorative designs, particularly since the table was probably originally located in the servants' wing, now our administrative offices, and would therefore not be exhibited to the public."

Exterior of Fallingwater (Edgar Kaufmann house), Mill Run, Pennsylvania, 1936.

Table

American black-walnut veneer over plywood
Designed for Fallingwater (Edgar Kaufmann house), Mill Run,
Pennsylvania
c. 1936
24 x 16 x 16 inches (61 x 40.6 x 40.6 cm)
1986.02.10

AULDBRASS PLANTATION

Yemassee, South Carolina, 1940

Wright developed the Usonian house to provide inexpensive housing for the average, middle-income family, and developed various ingenious innovations in the interests of economy. Yet Wright gave each client an individually designed house based on a modular unit often of hexagonal form initially used in 1936 for the Paul Hanna house. Auldbrass, designed for Leigh Stevens, is hexagonal and this is reflected in the furniture. Although complex in form, the construction of the table is relatively simple and inexpensive, thus satisfying Wright's Usonian ideal. The shape of the top is repeated in the architecture as seen in the plan; it consists of hexagonal modules joined to create interpenetrating planes. The table top was designed to fit together with two identical tables to produce a modular cluster. Although floor plans now owned by the Taliesin Foundation show these tables together, in later photographs they appear independently, perhaps a preference of the Stevens family. The angles of the table base correspond to the architectural structure that had slanting exterior walls placed at 80-degree angles to echo the landscape. Thus Wright's long interest in nature and his desire to build structures that reflect their environment is well evident in the Stevens commission. Made of cypress, a tree native to the South Carolina low country, this table was stained and waxed to reveal the natural wood and its beautiful graining. The interior walls of the house were also made of cypress and were similarly treated.

PRESERVATION NOTE

The fate of Auldbrass Plantation subsequent to its sale by the Stevens family has been one of steady deterioration. Most of the furnishings were either given to The Metropolitan Museum of Art in 1981 or sold at Sotheby's on November 19, 1981. Recently purchased by a new owner, Auldbrass is presently undergoing restoration.

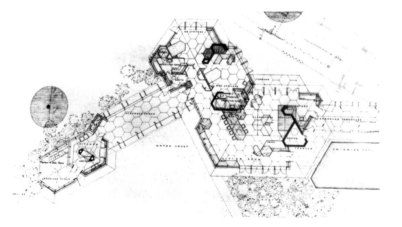

Plan of Auldbrass Plantation (Leigh Stevens house), Yemassee, South Carolina, 1940.

Center table

Cypress, laminated mahogany core
Designed for Auldbrass Plantation (Leigh Stevens house),
Yemassee, South Carolina
c. 1940
29½ x 59½ x 59½ inches (74.9 x 151.1 x 151.1 cm)
1986.05.04

Clerestory panel

Cypress, glass
Designed for Auldbrass Plantation (Leigh Stevens house),
Yemassee, South Carolina
c. 1940
11 ½ x 50 ¼ inches (29.3 x 127.7 cm)
1986.01.05

The clerestory panels in Wright's Usonian homes represented a measure of economy. They allowed wall space beneath for built-in furniture and bookshelves while admitting light to the interior from above; some of the panels were hinged to provide ventilation. The extensive Auldbrass Plantation included caretaker's and guest houses, a farm, and cottages for farm workers.

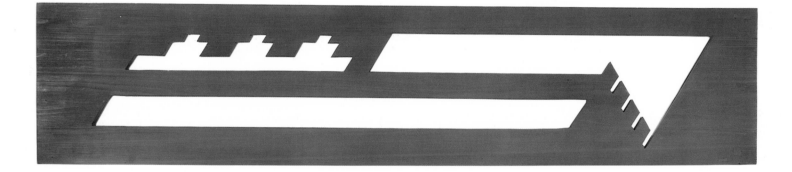

Exterior of Auldbrass Plantation (Leigh Stevens house),
Yemassee, South Carolina, 1940.

CLARENCE W. SONDERN HOUSE

Kansas City, Missouri, 1940

A typical Usonian house, the L-plan Sondern residence, despite its small size, provided a spacious living area. For the small bedrooms Wright designed compact, built-in furniture that was based on the same modular unit employed for the architecture and that was meant to be built on the job site by carpenters rather than in a more expensive cabinetmaking shop. Thus, although low in cost, the Usonian house contained furniture that was, according to Wright, "organic in character . . . that is, textures and patterns that sympathize in their own design and construction with the design and construction of the particular house they occupy." In the interests of economy, Wright developed innovations in the design of his Usonian furniture. For example, only one type of wood, cypress, was used throughout the Sondern interior and for the exterior as well. This was less expensive than oak and offered resistance to moisture. As a further economy, the subtle refinements of the well-crafted Prairie-style furniture, which required the skills of a cabinetmaker, were not attempted. In this Usonian chair the edges are unadorned and no moldings are used to create the richness of Wright's earlier furniture.

PRESERVATION NOTE

After World War II, the Sondern house was radically changed when new owners asked Wright to double its size. In 1986, much of its furniture was sold. As the original owners of houses built in the 1940s and 1950s have died, or the houses are sold, the original furniture tends to be dispersed, thus following the pattern for the Prairie houses whose furnishings were also sold or removed.

Interior of the Clarence W. Sondern house, Kansas City, Missouri, 1940.

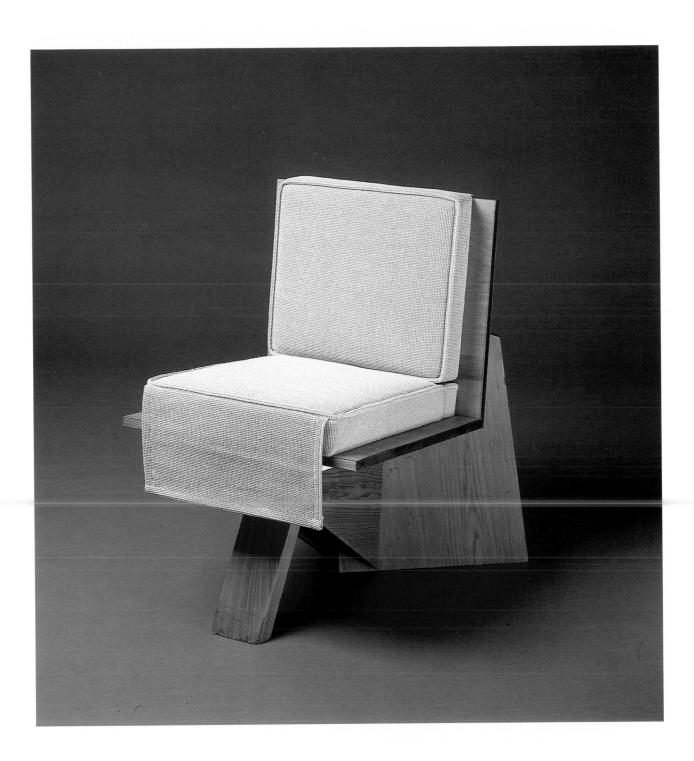

Side chair

Cypress, with upholstered seat and back cushions
Designed for the Clarence W. Sondern house, Kansas City, Missouri
c. 1940
28 x 22 x 22¼ inches (71 x 55.9 x 56.5 cm)
1986.02.04

TALIESIN WEST

Scottsdale, Arizona, 1946

Constructed as a prototype by Burton B. Busch of the Kapp Cabinet Shop, this chair form was originally designed for Wright's Taliesin West living room. A blueprint for this model, now in a private collection, is dated 1946. The arms convey the impression that they are hinged, and can possibly be folded, but in actuality they are stationary and braced with wedges from behind. This feature is in keeping with the "origami" or fold-up character of much of Wright's Usonian furniture. The standing "buttress" back also appears in the dining-room chairs that Wright designed in the same year for the Davis house in Marion, Indiana.

PRESERVATION NOTE

The original "origami" chairs are still preserved *in situ* at Taliesin West. Because it was the cabinetmaker's prototype, this chair was never part of any architectural interior, and therefore it is appropriate that it be included in a museum collection.

Living room of Taliesin West, Scottsdale, Arizona, 1932.

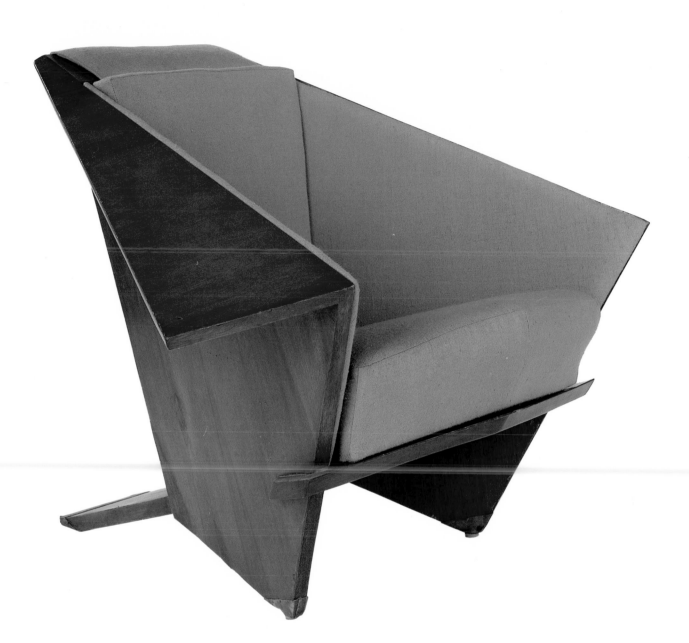

Armchair

Tropical hardwood, douglas fir, with upholstered seat and
back cushions
Designed for Taliesin West, Scottsdale, Arizona
c. 1946
30½ x 41⅛ x 36⅝ inches (77.4 x 104.3 x 93 cm)
Signed "BBB"
1986.01.04

Entrance of the New York Exhibition House, 1953, showing the clerestory panels.

Dining room of the New York Exhibition House, 1953.

NEW YORK EXHIBITION HOUSE

New York, New York, 1953

In *A Testament*, published in 1957, Wright described the derivation of the term *Usonian*:

> Samuel Butler, author of *The Way of All Flesh*, originator of the modern realistic novel, in his *Erehwon*, pitied us for having no name of our own. "The United States" did not appear to him a good title for us as a nation and the word "American" belonged to us only in common with a dozen or more countries. So he suggested USONIAN—roots of the word in the word *unity* or in *union*.

Although much Usonian furniture was standardized, designs for these clerestory panels varied from one commission to another. Recalling the leaded-glass window designs of the period before 1910, they contain integral decorative patterns. They are used in place of windows to light a passageway, and to suggest the thinness and penetrability of the exterior walls of the house. This particular panel was designed for the Usonian Pavilion, which was part of the exhibition "Sixty Years of Living Architecture," held in 1953 in New York City on the site where Wright's Solomon R. Guggenheim Museum now stands at Fifth Avenue and 89th Street.

PRESERVATION NOTE

In June 1984, Thomas Monaghan purchased at auction the remains of the entire Usonian house. Future plans at Domino's Farms include the exhibition of part of this house at The National Center for the Study of Frank Lloyd Wright.

Clerestory panel

Cypress
Designed for the New York Exhibition House
c. 1953
15¾ x 45¾ inches (40 x 116.2 cm)
1986.02.01

PAUL J. TRIER HOUSE

Des Moines, Iowa, 1956

Every aspect of furniture for a Usonian house was similarly designed. Wright described the furnishings appropriate for a Usonian house: "Rugs, draperies, and furnishings that are suitable for a Usonian house are those, too, that are organic in character; that is, textures and patterns that sympathize in their own design and construction with the design and construction of the particular house they occupy and embellish." This coffee table from the Trier house has many of the same qualities as the chairs from other Usonian commissions. The legs are basically planar elements that support upper and lower shelves that seem to hover as if suspended in space. This quality ultimately derives from Japanese architecture for which Wright had a lifetime fascination.

PRESERVATION NOTE

Furniture from the Trier house was sold in New York in 1986, and this table was purchased at that time.

Coffee table

Birch
Designed for the Paul J. Trier house, Des Moines, Iowa
c. 1956
18⅛ x 47⅞ x 47⅞ inches (46 x 121.5 x 121.5 cm)
1986.02.09

The side chairs from the Trier house follow the Usonian concept. The chair base has the same planar elements for leg supports, although juxtaposed in an unusual manner. If the perforated geometric ornament of the chair back seems, at first, to be more elaborate than in other Usonian furnishings, it will be remembered that Wright employed similar motifs in the base of his chairs for Paul R. Hanna, Palo Alto, California (1937), and in the clerestory panels of his Usonian houses. Identical dining chairs were originally designed for the Usonian Pavilion in 1953. Sometimes slight variations occurred and, as part of a custom interior, helped create an individual design for each client.

Side chair

Laminated birch, upholstered seat and back cushions
Designed for the Paul J. Trier house, Des Moines, Iowa
c. 1956
37⅛ x 18½ x 19½ inches (94.3 x 47 x 49.5 cm)
1986.02.08

HERITAGE-HENREDON FURNITURE

Morganton and High Point, North Carolina, 1955

Interior showing Heritage-Henredon furniture and F. Schumacher & Co. fabrics, 1955.

Simultaneous with textiles and wallpaper designed for F. Schumacher & Co., Wright developed a line of furniture for the Heritage-Henredon Furniture Company. Promoted in the November 1955 issue of *House Beautiful*, Wright's furniture was in sharp contrast to the predominance of period styles favored by Henredon. However, compared to furniture designs by Charles Eames of this same period, Wright's furniture is decidedly traditional in feeling. The Heritage line brought Wright-designed furniture to a wider public that could not afford to commission a complete house by the master. Although Wright designed three separate lines for Heritage-Henredon—the "Four Square," the "Honeycomb," and the "Burberry"—with each incorporating squares, triangles, and circles respectively, only the first, the most conservative of the three, was actually put into production.

Wright's designs for Heritage-Henredon, like his mass-produced Schumacher wallpaper and fabrics that were meant to accompany the furniture, are a departure from his typical working method. The designs from early in his career were made to fit a specific site, as well as economic and client requirements. The Heritage-Henredon ensembles were intended to be used in a more general way. According to the company's brochure, they represented "a thoughtful combination of natural mahogany, carved molding, and subtly-textured fabrics" made to create an atmosphere that would "complement any decorating scheme whether it be modern, Oriental, or Early American."

Although the furniture departed from Wright's ideal of an individualized interior, the Heritage-Henredon line was nonetheless based ultimately on the same principle as the furniture from early in his career. These furnishings were meant to create a feeling of integration and harmony and thus could be grouped and regrouped to meet different needs. In addition, the decorative vocabulary was present in the Prairie years. The ornamental molding that we see on much of Wright's Heritage-Henredon furniture served not only as decoration but also as structural emphasis and is not unlike what can be found on furnishings for the Husser and Bogk houses.

Table

Mahogany
Designed for the Heritage–Henredon Furniture Company,
Morganton and High Point, North Carolina
1955
26¼ x 29 x 25⅛ inches (66.6 x 73.7 x 63.9 cm)
1987.11.04

F. SCHUMACHER & CO.

New York, New York, 1955

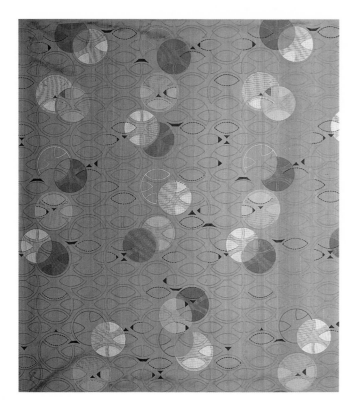

Among Wright's commercial endeavors was a series of fabrics and wallpapers called "The Taliesin Line" designed for F. Schumacher & Co. Made to accompany the Heritage-Henredon furniture, this line, like the furniture itself, was promoted in *House Beautiful* for November 1955. Both the fabrics and furniture made for mass production represent a distinct departure from the course followed in his early career, when he was concerned with designing furniture and decorative objects for specific interiors. Despite the fact that these fabrics were made to be mass produced, they were, however, meant to reflect Wright's main principle: that the decorative designs relate to the architectural scheme. Evidence for this is seen in a sample book, an example of which is in the Domino's Pizza Collection, *Schumacher's Taliesin Line of Decorative Fabrics and Wallpapers*. Here, wallpapers identical in design to the fabrics were recommended for use on a single wall in the same room where Heritage-Henredon furniture was included.

Like Wright's art glass, each of the printed fabrics for "The Taliesin Line" was conceived as a two-dimensional pattern in order to stress the planar nature of the material. Many of the designs, including No. 104, employ themes that Wright had been using throughout his career. His fondness for spherical motifs began as early as 1912 with the Coonley Playhouse windows, and it was used later in such buildings as Taliesin III in the mid-1930s. The design for this fabric was shown in the photographs of the bedroom of Schumacher's *Taliesin Suite*, where it was used for both wall-to-wall draperies and a quilted bedspread. Although shown in slate color in the Schumacher sample book, the fabric in the collection, available in six colors, is a multicolored abstract modular design based on the floor plans of residences designed for his sons Robert Llewellyn Wright and David Wright.

Fabric (Design No. 104)

Printed silk and Fortisan
Designed for F. Schumacher & Co., New York City
1955
117⅜ x 49¾ inches (298 x 126.4 cm)
1986.07.02

Textile (Design No. 102)

Printed linen
Designed for F. Schumacher & Co., New York
1955
83¾ x 46½ inches (212.7 x 118.1 cm)
1986.28.01

HAROLD C. PRICE CO. TOWER

Bartlesville, Oklahoma, 1956

The nineteen-story office-apartment building for the Harold C. Price Co. in Bartlesville, Oklahoma, was based on an earlier unexecuted plan made by Wright for the St. Mark's Tower in New York City in 1929. Wright felt that a skyscraper was unsuitable for an urban area if it increased congestion; therefore it should stand free in an open area. The Price Tower is a cantilevered steel building, a "treelike mast structure," embedded in concrete. All floors and walls are supported solely by four interior wall columns of steel-reinforced concrete. All furnishings were custom-designed for the building, including those for the two-story apartments. The tightness of plan and the angular rooms and furniture give the feeling of being on shipboard. The design of the tower and its furnishings is based on a diamond modular of 30-degree and 60-degree triangles. This design is seen scored on the floor as a pattern throughout the building. The interior wall supports divide the tower into four separate quadrants. The hexagonal back and vertical support were initially used in the chairs designed for the Imperial Hotel. The custom-designed upholstery related in pattern and color to the building.

Exterior of the Price Tower, Bartlesville, Oklahoma, 1956.

An apartment in the Price Tower, Bartlesville, Oklahoma, 1956.

Side chair

Aluminum, original upholstered seat and back
Designed for the Harold C. Price Co. Tower, Bartlesville, Oklahoma
c. 1956
32⅝ x 19 x 20¾ inches (82.9 x 48.3 x 52.7 cm)
1988.06.01

DONALD LOVNESS HOUSE

Stillwater, Minnesota, 1956

Among Wright's favorite clients from the 1950s were Donald and Virginia Lovness, who built their own house to the architect's specifications, including all the custom furnishings. Wright's continuing geometric-design sense is readily apparent in this gate that compares to a much earlier design of 1895 in wrought iron for the Francis Apartments in Chicago. The more symmetrical and rigid design for the Francis Apartments has now given way to an asymmetrical interpretation and is related to the gates designed for Taliesin West. The gate was manufactured by Victoria Welding, Victoria, Minnesota.

PRESERVATION NOTE

This gate was originally at the entrance to the Lovness property, and was removed in 1986 to prevent its deterioration and also for practical considerations, for its narrowness did not allow access by wider vehicles belonging to the owners. The stone footings and wall were also removed.

Exterior of the Donald Lovness house, Stillwater, Minnesota, 1956.

Gate *in situ*, Donald Lovness house, Stillwater, Minnesota, 1956.

Pair of gates

Wrought iron, painted red
Designed for the Donald Lovness house, Stillwater, Minnesota
c. 1956
Each section: 51 ½ x 62 x 6 inches (130.8 x 157.4 x 15.2 cm)
1986.23.68a,b

GRAPHIC DESIGN

In *An Autobiography*, Wright described his lifelong interest in graphic design. As a child, he had set up a small printing press and, as he said, came "to love the smell of printer's ink." In 1896, Wright worked with two clients, William H. Winslow and Chauncy L. Williams, who purchased type and a large handpress and established the Auvergne Press. Their first work, published in December 1896, was John Keats's poem *Eve of St. Agnes*. The only other title, *The House Beautiful* by William C. Gannet, was published in a small edition of ninety copies. The style of the title page reflects the work of William Morris in the lavish detailing and of Wright's mentor, Louis Sullivan, in the refined abstracted design based on naturalistic forms. The book is composed of a series of intricate pen-and-ink drawings in Wright's own hand. Many of the designs utilize an entire page and are reminiscent of Oriental carpets that Wright admired and used. The pages, with wide decorative margins surrounding a text, reflect an Arts and Crafts ideology. In the book one sees that Wright drew in a naturalistic as well as in an abstract manner. Here a repeated male figure holds a square block, a device used in Wright's own signature, and walks in a stylized landscape. The metaphor illustrates the process by which the architect derives his geometric sense of design from nature. This process of stylizing a motif was the basis for Wright's ornament.

PRESERVATION NOTE

Examples of the ninety published copies of *The House Beautiful* can be found in American libraries, among them the Avery Library at Columbia University and the Chicago Historical Society. Because of the high quality of the paper used, many of these copies remain in good condition.

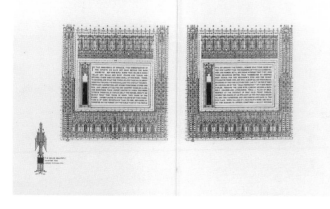

Two pages from the second chapter of *The House Beautiful*, 1897.

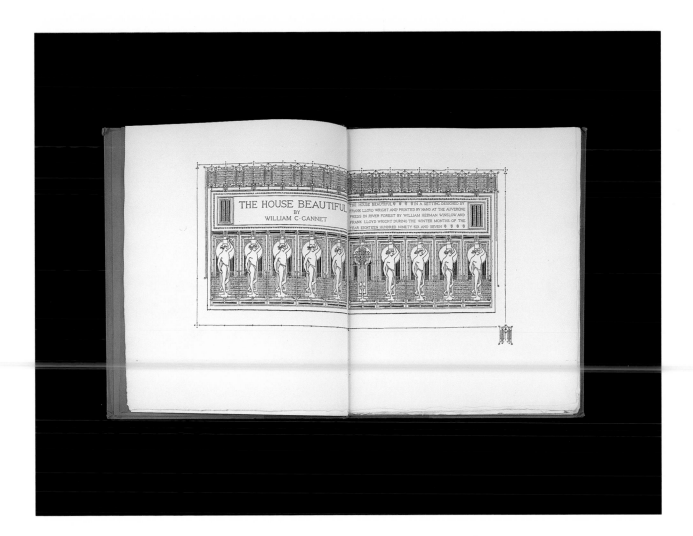

Book, opened to title page

The House Beautiful
Published by the Auvergne Press, River Forest, Illinois
1897
This copy is numbered "5/90" and signed in ink in script on the
last page, "W.H. Winslow/Frank Lloyd Wright."
Closed: 14 x 11¾ inches (35.6 x 29.8 cm)
1986.23.95

Six drawings

Pencil and crayon on paper
Designs for *Liberty* magazine covers
c. 1927
JANUARY: 13½ x 23½ inches (34.3 x 59.7 cm), 1986.08.02
FEBRUARY: 14¼ x 24 inches (36.2 x 60.1 cm), 1986.29.02
MARCH: 14³⁄₁₆ x 24 inches (36 x 60.1 cm), 1986.08.01
APRIL: 14⅛ x 24 inches (35.9 x 60.1 cm), 1986.29.01
JUNE: 14 x 23⅞ inches (35.6 x 60 cm), 1986.29.03
DECEMBER: 14⅛ x 24¼ inches (35.9 x 61.6 cm), 1986.08.03

Wright's interest in graphic design continued throughout his career. In 1926–1927, he designed twelve covers for *Liberty* magazine, one for each month; none, however, was published by the magazine. These exquisite drawings attest to his superb draughtsmanship and skill as a graphic designer. Each cover design suggests a particular month. In the January design, for example, he incorporated elements suggestive of icicles. His keen eye for harmonious color is also evident in a palette that changed through the years. The style of these designs is an extension of the architect's exploration of nonobjective imagery begun in the Coonley Playhouse windows of 1912, and may well have been influenced by paintings by Frantisek Kupka and Robert Delaunay that he could have seen in 1910 in Paris. The intricate compositions of triangles, squares, and circles seen in these wonderful drawings are also found in other works by Wright, most notably in the mural for the living-room fireplace in Aline Barnsdall's Hollyhock House of 1920.

PRESERVATION NOTE

These six drawings in the collection descended to Wright's granddaughter and were subsequently sold. The drawing for May is now in a private collection. Others in the series are in the Taliesin West archives and at The Museum of Modern Art, New York. Restoration of these drawings has been carried out by paper conservation specialists at the Detroit Institute of Arts, Detroit, Michigan.

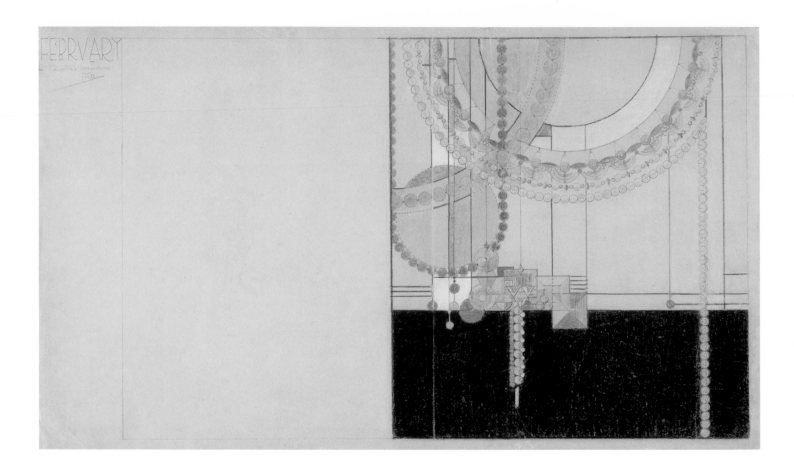

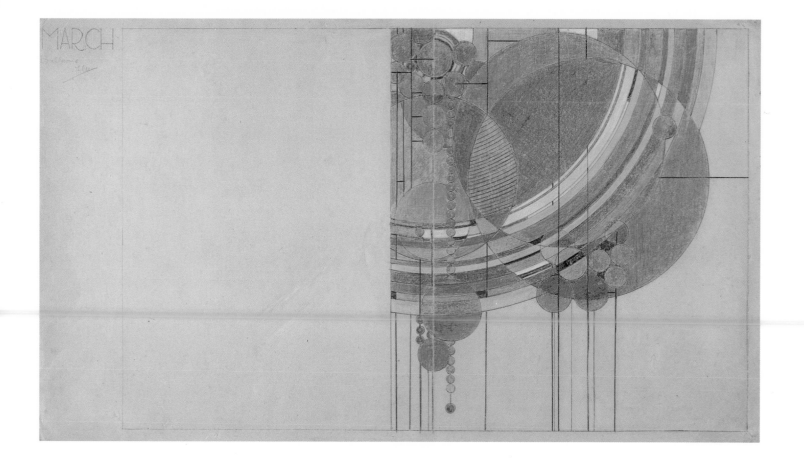

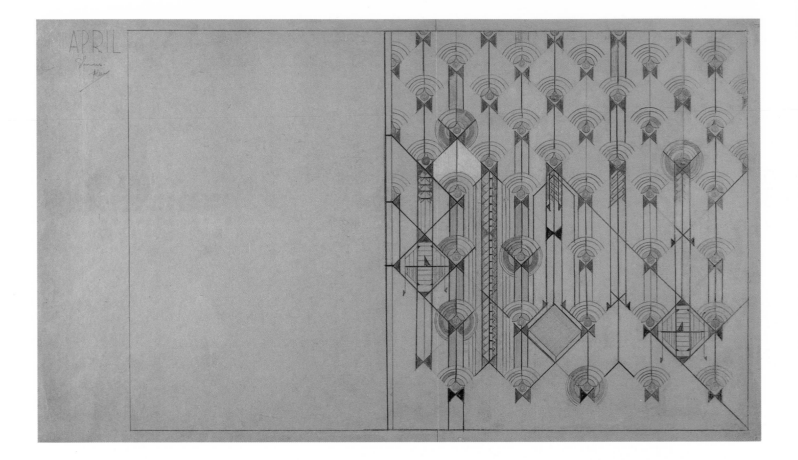

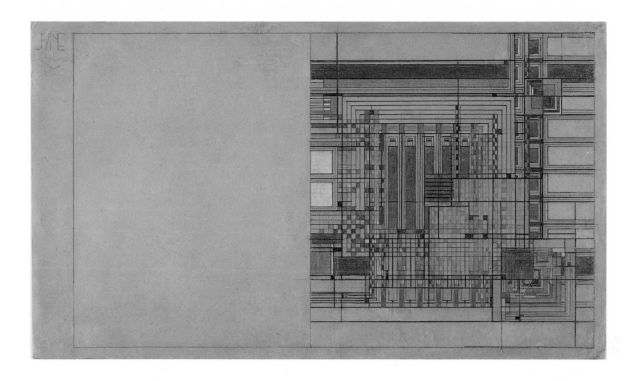

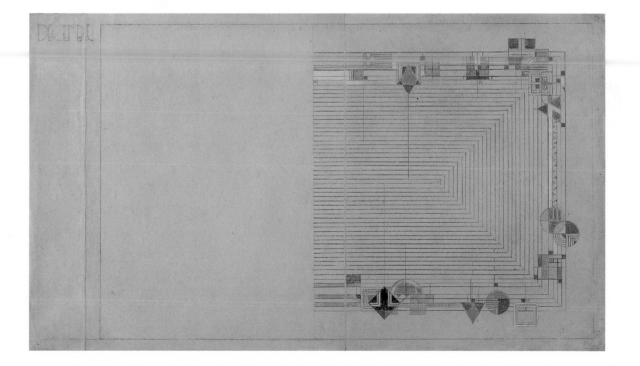

Book, open to "Book Two—Work"

An Autobiography, published by Longmans, Green, and Company
1932
Closed: 9⅛ x 7½ inches (23.2 x 19 cm)
1986.23.100

Wright's design for "Work" illustrates his architectural principle of continuity because the "plowed field" motif is continued into Book Three. Wright's *An Autobiography* was praised in a contemporary review as a book "that compares in brilliance and originality with his buildings . . ." The design of the book marks a stylistic progress from *The House Beautiful* of 1897, where a tight linearity has given way here to a more rigorous geometric pattern. Wright wrote the following about his nonobjective abstract designs for the book:

> This principle of design was natural, inevitable for me. Whether in glass or textile or whatever, it is based on the straight-line technique of the T square and the triangle. It was inherent in the Froebel system of kindergarten training given me by my mother—for I built many designs and buildings on the kitchen table out of the geometric forms of those playthings. Out of this came the straight-line patterns that are used today in textiles, linoleums and so on. But it grew out of my own limitations, by way of the T square and the triangle and the compass.

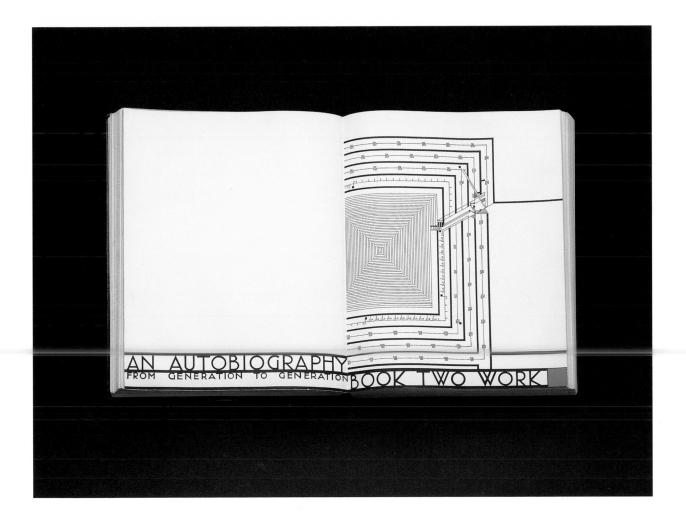

Cover

Town and Country magazine
July 1937
13 ½ x 9¾ inches (34.3 x 24.7 cm)
1986.23.106

One of Wright's most exuberant graphic designs was created for and used on the July 1937 cover of *Town and Country*. Appropriately, the American flag was the theme; in reverse at the right and conventionally in the center. Wright's playful variations on the flag motif give depth to the composition and create the impression of a street, and this impression is strengthened by the flags hanging at an angle. The flags are superimposed on a vertical grid, so the overall effect is one of exciting movement in an elegant and dynamic composition.

Town & Country

ESTABLISHED 1846

JULY 1937
PRICE 50 CENTS
DESIGNED BY FRANK LLOYD WRIGHT

CHECKLIST

This checklist is divided into the following sections: designs by Wright, graphic designs and books by Wright, and works by other designers. The dates given are those of the design of the house or project. Although Wright conceived his buildings as a whole and sketches for furniture were sometimes drawn concurrent to or within the same year as the architectural plans, the studio would not begin the working drawings for the furniture until the house was being built. When a significant variation in dating between the design of the architecture and decorative arts is documented, the alternate date is also listed. Dimensions are in inches, followed by centimeters; height precedes width and depth. Original framing and upholstery are noted; measurements of windows are without frame, unless framing is original.

DESIGNS BY FRANK LLOYD WRIGHT

(Listed alphabetically by client or commission)

American Luxfer Prism Company

Chicago, Illinois, patented October 4, 1897

Two windows
Molded glass in original frames
Each: 36 x 79 inches
91.4 x 200.7 cm
86.34.03,4

Loose blocks
Molded glass
Each block: 4 x 4 inches
10 x 10 cm
86.42.01

The Art Institute of Chicago Exhibition Japanese print show

Chicago, Illinois, March 1908

Print stand (similar to one used in the Art Institute exhibition)
Mahogany, Japanese print (not original to stand)
35½ x 8⅝ x 10⅝ inches
90 x 22 x 27 cm
86.08.13

Aline Barnsdall Hollyhock House

Los Angeles, California, 1920

Window
Leaded glass
71¼ x 6 inches
181 x 15.2 cm
86.08.11

Lantern
Bronze and textured glass
19½ x 7 x 7¼ inches
49.5 x 17.8 x 18.4 cm
86.08.12

Specifications (two typed pages)
Paper
8½ x 11 inches
21.6 x 27.9 cm
86.23.55

Fabric sample
1¾ x 2½ inches
4.5 x 6.4 cm
86.23.56a

Fabric sample
2⅝ x 4¾ inches
6.7 x 12.1 cm
86.23.56b

Fabric sample
2¾ x 1¾ inches
7 x 4.5 cm
86.23.56c

Blueprint: front and side elevations and plan of easy chair and stool for living room
14¾ x 19⅞ inches
37.5 x 50.5 cm
86.23.59

Blueprint: front and side elevations for dining room chair and detail of table leg
Dated May 1921
11⅞ x 20½ inches
30.3 x 52 cm
86.23.60

Blueprint: plan of first floor and
surrounding grounds
August 16 and September 1920,
signed "FLW"
Additional revisions in colored pencil
23¾ x 28½ inches
60.3 x 72.4 cm
86.23.61

Blueprint: side and front elevations
and plans for couch/table and foot stool
for living room
18¾ x 29¼ inches
47.6 x 74.3 cm
86.23.62

Blueprint: living-room rug
Dated March 10, 1921, with notation in
pencil
19½ x 25⅝ inches
49.5 x 65.1 cm
86.23.63

Blueprint: front and side elevation of
loggia chair
11¾ x 21½ inches
29.8 x 54.6 cm
86.23.107

Peter A. Beachy House

Oak Park, Illinois, 1906

Sconce
Bronze, leaded glass, and oak
8⅞ x 4⅜ x 7¼ inches
22.5 x 11.2 x 18.1 cm
86.05.03

B. Harley Bradley House: Glenlloyd

Kankakee, Illinois, 1900

Pair of casement windows
Leaded glass in original frames
Each: 38⅞ x 19½ inches
98.6 x 49.5 cm
86.05.01a,b

Pair of casement windows
Leaded glass in original frames
Each: 35¾ x 18 inches
90.8 x 45.7 cm
86.05.02a,b

Pair of casement windows and transom
Leaded glass in original frames
Pair, each: 41 x 21¾ inches
104 x 55.2 cm
Transom: 17¾ x 43¼ inches
45.1 x 109.9 cm
86.06.01a–c

Pair of dining room cabinet doors
Leaded glass in original frames
Each: 45⅛ x 22¼ inches
104.9 x 56.6 cm
86.06.02,3

Window
Leaded glass in original frame
42⅞ x 17½ inches
109 x 44.5 cm
86.34.07

Window
Leaded glass in original frame
33½ x 16¼ inches
85.1 x 41.3 cm
86.34.08

Serving table
Oak, brass pulls
40¾ x 36 x 21½ inches
103.5 x 91.4 x 54.6 cm
87.17.03

Avery Coonley House

Riverside, Illinois, 1907

Window
Leaded glass
44½ x 23½ inches
112.4 x 59.7 cm
85.01.04

Three windows
Leaded glass
Each: 32 x 20⅛ inches
81.2 x 51 cm
85.01.05–7

*Rendering of stables and
gardener's cottage*
Pencil and colored pencil on tissue
5½ x 19½ inches
14 x 49.5 cm
86.20.03

Two windows
Leaded glass
Each: 29⅜ x 14 inches
74.7 x 35.5 cm
Framed together: 35 x 37¼ inches
80.9 x 90.5 cm
86.20.04a,b

Bank of eight interior corridor windows
Leaded glass in original frame
Each: 10 x 10½ inches
25.4 x 26.7 cm
Framed together: 25⁵⁄₁₆ x 48¼ inches
64.8 x 122.6 cm
86.20.05

Two sconces
Bronze, frosted glass globes, mica
Each: 7¼ x 11 x 9 inches
18.4 x 28 x 22.8 cm
86.20.06,7

Side chair
Oak, upholstered slip seat
39⅛ x 14⅞ x 18¾ inches
99.4 x 37.7 x 47.6 cm
87.17.14

Two side chairs
Oak, upholstered slip seats
Each: 37 x 14¼ x 16¼ inches
94 x 36.2 x 41.3 cm
87.17.16, 17

Window
Leaded glass
31¼ x 19¼ inches
79.4 x 48.9 cm
87.17.18

Library table
Oak
38⅞ x 65¼ x 28¼ inches
101.3 x 165.7 x 71.7 cm
87.17.18

Two ceiling grilles
Oak
Each: 36½ x 7 inches
92.7 x 17.8 cm
88.05.02

Avery Coonley Playhouse

Riverside, Illinois, 1912

Two side chairs (adult version)
Birch, with leather-covered slip-seat
and back
Each: 34⅛ x 16 x 17⅜ inches
86.4 x 40.6 x 44.1 cm
85.02.02,3

Side chair (child's version)
Birch, with leather-covered slip-seat
and back
31 x 15¼ x 16⅜ inches
78.7 x 38.7 x 41.5 cm
85.02.04

Window
Leaded glass
60½ x 12½ inches
153.7 x 31.8 cm
86.06.05

Two windows
Leaded glass
Each: 6⅜ x 14⅞ inches
16.5 x 38 cm
86.06.06,7

Triptych of windows
Leaded glass in original frame
Framed ensemble: 40½ x 64½ inches
102.8 x 165 cm
86.25.01a–c

Window
Leaded glass in original frame
35⅜ x 7⅞ inches
89.9 x 20 cm
85.25.02

Window
Leaded glass in original frame
36¾ x 7⅞ inches
92.4 x 20 cm
86.25.03

Window
Leaded glass in original frame
38 x 7¹¹⁄₁₆ inches
96.5 x 19.8 cm
86.25.04

Window
Leaded glass in original frame
35⁵⁄₁₆ x 7¹¹⁄₁₆ inches
89.7 x 19.8 cm
86.25.05

Window
Leaded glass in original frame
43⅞ x 6⁹⁄₁₆ inches
111.3 x 16.65 cm
86.25.06

Window
Leaded glass in original frame
44⅜ x 6⅝ inches
112.5 x 16.9 cm
86.25.07

Twenty clerestory windows
Leaded glass in original frames
Each: 24 x 38⅜ inches
61 x 97.5 cm
86.25.08–27

Two windows
Leaded glass
Each: 25 x 34 inches
63.5 x 86.4 cm
86.29.04,5

Susan Lawrence Dana House

Springfield, Illinois, 1902

Frieze fragment
Painted plaster
28¼ x 28 inches
71.8 x 71 cm
86.36.01

Urn, designed c. 1895–1900
This example made c. 1902
Sheet copper
19 x 19 x 19 inches
48.2 x 48.2 x 48.2 cm
85.04.01

Ray W. Evans House

Chicago, Illinois, 1908

Two armchairs
Oak
Each: 34¼ x 30¼ x 24 inches
87 x 76.8 x 61 cm
86.08.04,5

Four dining chairs
Oak, with leather-covered slip seats
Each: 44¾ x 15⅜ x 18⅜ inches
113.5 x 39.1 x 46.6 cm
86.40.01–4

Florida Southern College

Lakeland, Florida, 1938–1954

Building block (reproduced in 1970)
Cement
9 x 36 x 3¼ inches
22.9 x 91.4 x 8.3 cm
86.10.01

Samuel Freeman House

Los Angeles, California, 1923

Twenty-four building blocks (1987
reproductions from the original molds)
Three varieties (six plain, six with
perforations and patterns, twelve with
patterns only)
Concrete
Each: 16 x 16 x 3½ inches
40 x 40 x 8.75 cm
87.14.01

Geneva Inn

Lake Geneva, Wisconsin, 1911

Window
Leaded glass in original frame
48¾ x 22⅝ inches
123.7 x 57.5 cm
85.01.02

Window
Leaded glass in original frame
48⅞ x 24½ inches
124.2 x 62.2 cm
85.01.03

Two windows
Leaded glass in original frame
Each: 48¾ x 22⅜ inches
123.9 x 57 cm
85.03.03,4

Two windows
Leaded glass in original frame
Each: 49 x 32½ inches
124.5 x 82.6 cm
86.23.46,47

Lantern
Textured and frosted glass, brass
8⅝ x 9 x 9 inches
21.9 x 22.8 x 22.8 cm
86.23.96

William A. Greene House

Aurora, Illinois, 1912

Sideboard
Oak
46 x 82¾ x 17⅝ inches
116.8 x 210 x 44.9 cm
86.08.06

Settle
Oak, with leather-covered seat cushion
30½ x 80 x 32¾ inches
77.5 x 203.0 x 83.2 cm
86.18.01

Isidore H. Heller House

Chicago, Illinois, 1897

Eaves panel
Wood with traces of original paint
38½ x 9½ inches
97.8 x 24.1 cm
87.15.01

Capital
Molded plaster, painted
Each half: 15⅞ x 20¼ x 9⅝ inches
38.4 x 52 x 24.5 cm
88.03.01a,b

Heritage-Henredon Furniture Company

Morganton and High Point, North Carolina, 1955

Dining table with two extension leaves (#2002)
Mahogany
28½ x 63⅝ x 42 inches
72.4 x 161.6 x 106.7 cm
Each leaf: 18 x 42 inches
45.7 x 106.7 cm
85.05.01a–c

Dining chairs (two armchairs and four side chairs, #2000)
Mahogany, upholstered seats and backs
Each armchair: 39⅞ x 22 x 24⅜ inches
101.3 x 55.9 x 61.9 cm
Each sidechair: 39⅞ x 19⅞ x 23 inches
101.3 x 50.5 x 58.4 cm
85.05.02–7

Planter: designed for Minic Accessories, New York City, to accompany the Heritage-Henredon furniture line
Mahogany, copper paint
4 x 22⅝ x 12⅝ inches
10.2 x 57.5 x 32.1 cm
86.02.11

Sideboard (#2000)
Mahogany
"FLW" in square stamped on back
33 x 65½ x 20 inches
83.8 x 166.4 x 50.8 cm
86.11.01

Vase: designed for Minic Accessories, New York City, to accompany the Heritage-Henredon furniture line
Mahogany, copper insert
44⅛ x 11½ x 11½ inches
112.1 x 29.2 x 29.2 cm
86.12.01

Two end tables (#2000)
Mahogany
"FLW" in square stamped on back of each
Each: 28½ x 21⅜ x 20 inches
71.4 x 54.3 x 50.8 cm
86.13.01,2

Sideboard (#2000)
Mahogany
"FLW" in square stamped on back
34⅞ x 66 x 20 inches
88.7 x 167.6 x 50.8 cm
86.14.01

Dining table with extension leaf (#2001)
Mahogany, copper trim
Without leaf, 24³⁄₁₆ x 54 (diameter) inches
61.5 x 137 cm
Leaf: 54 x 12 inches
137 x 30.5 cm
86.30.01a,b

Eight dining chairs (#2001)
Mahogany, upholstered seats and backs
Each: 27⅜ x 20½ x 22¾ inches
69.6 x 52.1 x 57.8 cm
86.30.02–9

Breakfront (composed of "China Deck," #2006 and "Triple Dresser Base," #2000)
Mahogany
78¼ x 61⅜ x 20 inches
198.4 x 155.9 x 50.8 cm
86.33.01

Table (#451-L)
Mahogany
26¼ x 29 x 25⅛ inches
66.7 x 73.7 x 63.9 cm
87.11.04

Pair of stacking cocktail tables (#452-C)
Mahogany
Stamped on bottom "HH Heritage Henredon/Frank Lloyd Wright"
Each: 12¼ x 26½ x 26½ inches
31.1 x 67.3 x 67.3 cm
87.11.02,3

Couch in two sections ("Left Bumper sectional," #1579 and "Right Bumper sectional," #1580)
Mahogany, upholstered seat and back
Each section: 30½ x 61¼ x 28⅛ inches
77.5 x 155.6 x 71.9 cm
87.11.01a,b

Arthur Heurtley House

Oak Park, Illinois, 1902

Two reclining armchairs
Birch, elm, with leather-covered cushions
Each: 37 x 32⅜ x 29½ inches
94 x 82.2 x 74.8 cm
86.01.01,2

Warren Hickox House

Kankakee, Illinois, 1900

Four clerestory windows
Leaded glass in original frames
Each: 25³⁄₁₆ x 22 inches
64 x 55.9 cm
87.06.01a,b
87.06.02a,b

Pair of doors
Leaded glass in original frames
Each: 79⅝ x 22⅛ inches
202.3 x 56.3 cm
87.06.03a,b

Side chair
Oak, leather-covered slip-seat
51 x 18½ x 19¾ inches
129.6 x 46.9 x 50.3 cm
87.15.02

Hillside Home School

Spring Green, Wisconsin, 1902

Two side chairs
Oak, original leather-covered slip-seats
Each: 39¼ x 15 x 19¼ inches
99.6 x 38 x 50.5 cm
86.34.05,6

Joseph W. Husser House

Chicago, Illinois, 1899

Dining table and eight side chairs
Oak, chairs with leather-covered slip-seats
Each chair: 51⅞ x 17¼ x 17¼ inches
131.8 x 43.8 x 43.8 cm
Table: 28 x 54 x 60 inches
71.1 x 137.2 x 152.4 cm
87.13.01 (table)
87.13.02–9 (chairs)

Imperial Hotel

Tokyo, Japan, 1916–1922

Side chair, designed c. 1921
This example made c. 1930
Oak, with original oil cloth-covered slip-seat and back
38 x 15¾ x 20 inches
96.5 x 40 x 51 cm
86.01.03

Architectural ornament
Terra-cotta
8½ x 8¼ x 2½ inches
21.6 x 21 x 6.3 cm
86.23.43

Architectural ornament
Terra-cotta
9 x 3¼ inches
22.9 x 8.3 cm
86.23.44

Carpet fragment
Wool
17 x 8¼ inches
43.2 x 21 cm
86.23.45

Place setting with tea service (17 pieces)
This set was used in the hotel after 1951
but was not designed by Frank Lloyd
Wright.
Glazed porcelain, rattan handles
Mark: Printed on bottom of
luncheon plates, "Noritake-China/
NIPPON TOKI KAISHA/1951"; other
pieces variously marked
Diameter of dinner plate: 8⅞ inches
22.6 cm
86.34.02

Side chair, designed c. 1921
This example made c. 1940–1950
Oak, Naugahyde-covered slip-seat and
back
37½ x 15 x 17⅞ inches
95.2 x 38 x 45.4 cm
86.34.09

Six salad plates, made 1961
Glazed porcelain
Each: 8 inches (diameter)
20.3 cm
87.09.01–6

*Place setting with cup, saucer, two bowls,
two plates,* made 1964–1966
Glazed porcelain
Each plate marked on bottom "Nori-
take/N/NIPPON TOKI KAISHA/JAPAN/1962"
(variously dated)
Plate: 7⅝ inches (diameter)
19.4 cm
Plate: 6⁷⁄₁₆ inches (diameter)
16.3 cm
Bowl: 1¹¹⁄₁₆ x 5¾ inches (diameter)
14.6 x 4.3 cm
Bowl: 1³⁄₁₆ x 5³⁄₁₆ inches (diameter)
13.2 x 3 cm
Saucer: 5⁵⁄₁₆ inches (diameter)
13.5 cm
Cup: 2³⁄₁₆ x 4³⁄₁₆ x 3⁷⁄₁₆ inches
5.5 x 10.5 x 8.8 cm
87.16.01–6

E.P. Irving House

Decatur, Illinois, 1910

Two pairs of windows
Leaded glass in original frames
Each window: 50⅛ x 19⅛ inches
127.3 x 48.6 cm
86.32.02a,b
86.32.03a,b

Plans showing first-floor furniture
placement
Pencil and watercolor on paper
Dated October 22, 1909
40½ x 24½ inches
102.9 x 62.2 cm
86.32.04

Edgar Kaufmann House: Fallingwater

Mill Run, Pennsylvania, 1936

Table
American black walnut veneer over
plywood
24 x 16 x 16 inches
61 x 40.6 x 40.6 cm
86.02.10

Larkin Company Administration Building

Buffalo, New York, 1904

Folding side chair
Painted steel, with leather-covered slip-
seat and back, castors
37 x 20⅛ x 20⅛ inches
94 x 51.1 x 51.1 cm
86.06.08

Side chair
Painted steel, upholstered slip-seat,
castors
36⅝ x 16⅞ x 14⅛ inches
93.1 x 42.9 x 35.8 cm
86.06.09

Armchair
Painted steel, with original leather-
covered seat, castors
38 x 24½ x 21 inches
96.5 x 61.6 x 53.3 cm
88.02.01

Desk with attached chair
Painted steel
43⅛ x 48⅛ x 24 inches
108.4 x 122.2 x 61 cm
88.01.01

Lawrence Memorial Library

Springfield, Illinois, 1905

Side chair
Oak, with upholstered slip-seat
29⅝ x 19¼ x 19⅜ inches
75.2 x 48.9 x 49.3 cm
87.17.04

Francis W. Little House

Peoria, Illinois, 1903

Window
Leaded glass in original frame
41¾ x 31⅝ inches
106 x 80.3 cm
85.01.01

Plan: house and grounds
Pencil and gilt ink on paper
Dated August 1904
12 x 33 inches
30.4 x 83.8 cm
86.23.15

Rendering
Pencil on paper
9¼ x 23⅛ inches
23.5 x 58.8 cm
86.23.16

Plan: first floor
Pencil and colored pencil on paper
11⅞ x 16 inches
30.1 x 40.6 cm
86.23.19

Plan: second floor with rug details
Pencil and ink on paper
12 x 16¼ inches
30.5 x 41.3 cm
86.23.20

Blueprint: elevations and details
26¾ x 43⅞ inches
67.9 x 111.4 cm
86.23.21

Elevation: iron railing
Pencil on paper
16¼ x 14⅞ inches
41.4 x 38 cm
86.23.27

Five side chairs
Oak, with original leather-covered
slip-seats
Each: 30 x 15¾ x 18⅛ inches
76.3 x 40 x 46 cm
86.23.34–38

Side chair
Oak, with original leather-covered
slip-seat
39 x 16 x 18½ inches
99.1 x 40.6 x 47 cm
86.23.40

Two side chairs, 1906
Mahogany, with original upholstered
slip-seats
Each: 27⅛ x 15⅞ x 17¼ inches
68.9 x 40.3 x 43.9 cm
86.23.41,42

Sconce
Brass-plated bronze, opalescent glass
13½ x 5 x 4¾ inches
34.3 x 12.7 x 12.1 cm
86.23.48

Dressing table, 1906
Mahogany, mahogany veneer, mirror,
brass pulls
Mirror dated 1906
56 x 46 x 20 inches
142.2 x 116.8 x 50.8 cm
86.23.49

Standing sconce
Brass plated bronze, opalescent glass
10⅛ x 4⅞ x 4⅞ inches
25.7 x 12.5 x 12.5 cm
86.23.70

Chest of drawers
Oak, brass pulls
70⅛ x 22⅞ x 27⅝ inches
178 x 50.8 x 70.1 cm
87.10.03

Reclining armchair
Oak, upholstered seat cushion
40 x 31¾ x 26¾ inches
101.6 x 80.6 x 67.9 cm
87.10.04

Window
Leaded glass
35⅜ x 26½ inches
90 x 67.3 cm
87.10.05

Armchair
Oak, upholstered seat cushion
23 x 26¾ x 25 inches
50.8 x 60.8 x 60.3 cm
87.10.06

Elevation, detail, and half plan of fireplace
Pencil and colored pencil on paper
30¾ x 28¼ inches
78.1 x 71.8 cm
86.23.108

Pair of beds
Oak
Each: 25¼ x 79 x 40⅛ inches
64 x 200.7 x 102 cm
87.17.05,6

Window
Leaded glass
12¾ x 4¼ inches
32.4 x 10.8 cm
87.17.07

Pair of windows
Leaded glass
Each: 35⅜ x 26½ inches
90 x 67.3 cm
87.17.08,9

Secretary
Oak, mirror, brass pulls
69¼ x 19 x 21¼ inches
175.9 x 48.3 x 54 cm
87.17.10

Side chair
Oak, upholstered slip-seat
39 x 15⅞ x 18¾ inches
99 x 40.2 x 47.7 cm
87.17.11

Francis W. Little House: Northome
Wayzata, Minnesota, 1912

Master bedroom
Including windows, masonary, wood
panels, door frames, flooring, lighting
fixtures
86.04.01

Pair of doors
Leaded glass in original frame and
surround
78 x 42 x 7¾ inches
198.2 x 106.7 x 19.8 cm
86.04.02

*Six clerestory windows from master
bedroom hallway*
Leaded glass in original frames
Each: 28¼ x 23¼ inches
71.8 x 59.1 cm
86.19.01–6

Bedroom
Various architectural elements and
windows, pair of beds, with attached
benches, and lighting fixtures
86.21.01

*Elevations of living-room furniture: table,
light table and chairs, pedestal, and davenport*
Pencil and colored pencil on paper
19⅜ x 40 inches
49.2 x 101.6 cm
86.23.01

Elevation of summer dwelling
Pencil and colored pencil on paper and
tissue paper overlay
16½ x 41¼ inches
41.9 x 104.8 cm
86.23.02

Elevations (front and side) of office furniture
Pencil on paper
15¾ x 24¼ inches
40 x 61.6 cm
86.23.03

Drawing of art-glass windows
Pencil and colored pencil on paper
15⅛ x 8¹/₁₆ inches
38.3 x 20.4 cm
86.23.04

Drawing of art-glass windows
Pencil and colored pencil on paper
Dated August 25, 1913
12⅞ x 21 inches
32.8 x 53.3 cm
86.23.05

*Elevations of living-room furniture: table,
screen, armchair and desk*
Pencil and colored pencil on paper
19⅛ x 40 inches
48.6 x 101.6 cm
86.23.06

Elevations of side brackets and lanterns
Pencil and colored pencil on paper
33½ x 14 inches
85.1 x 35.6 cm
86.23.07

Elevation of girder with detail
Pencil and colored pencil on paper
14⅛ x 35⅞ inches
35.9 x 91 cm
86.23.08

Sketch of plan
Pencil and colored pencil on graph
paper
7¾ x 9⅞ inches
19.7 x 25.2 cm
86.23.09

Sketch of plan: (with second sketch on verso)
Pencil on graph paper
7¾ x 9⅞ inches
19.7 x 25.2 cm
86.23.10

Sketch of plan: inception drawing for
Little residence
Pencil and colored pencil on graph
paper
7⅞ x 8⅝ inches
20.1 x 22 cm
86.23.11

Preliminary sketch: elevation and plan
Pencil on graph paper
8⅛ x 10½ inches
20.6 x 26.7 cm
86.23.12

Blueprint: first-floor plan
With pencil and colored pencil alterations
and revisions
Dated "Aug. 1912/Feb 1913/March"
22⅝ x 41⅞ inches
57.6 x 106.5 cm
86.23.13

Preliminary plan for Little cottage
Pencil on paper
16⅞ x 19 inches
42.8 x 48.3 cm
86.23.17

Preliminary elevations for Little cottage
Pencil on paper
17⅛ x 43½ inches
43.5 x 110.5 cm
86.23.18

Elevation and plan for cottage, fence, and gate; elevation and plan on verso
Pencil on graph paper
15¹⁵⁄₁₆ x 20⅞ inches
40.5 x 53 cm
86.23.23

Plan for landscaping, "Scheme A"
Pencil on paper
19½ x 15⅜ inches
49.5 x 39 cm
86.23.24

Plan: fireplace wall with detail on reverse
Pencil on graph paper, with notations
20⅞ x 15⅞ inches
53 x 40.3 cm
86.23.25

Blueprint: basement plan
Dated August 1912,
23 x 41⅛ inches
58.4 x 104.4 cm
86.23.26a, Bound together with b, c,
and d

Blueprint: first-floor plan
Dated August 1912,
23 x 41⅛ inches
58.4 x 104.4 cm
86.23.26b, Bound together with a, c,
and d

Blueprint: elevations
Dated August 1912,
23 x 41⅛ inches
58.4 x 104.4 cm
86.23.26c, bound together with a, b,
and d

Blueprint: sections
Dated August 1912
23 x 41⅛ inches
58.4 x 104.4 cm
86.23.26d, bound together with a, b,
and c

Specifications for summer cottage (five
typed pages)
Tissue, bound with card and metal studs
9½ x 8¼ inches
24.2 x 21.1 cm
86.23.28

Specifications for windows for summer dwelling (four typed pages)
Tissue, bound with kraft paper and
metal studs
7⅜ x 8⅝ inches
18.7 x 21.9 cm
86.23.29

Hall closet
Oak, maple interior
53¼ x 120 x 18¾ inches
135.3 x 304.8 x 47.6 cm
86.23.30

Hall closet
Oak, maple interior
53¼ x 48½ x 18¾ inches
135.3 x 123.2 x 47.6 cm
86.23.31

Door to hallway closet
Oak
76 x 21¾ inches
193 x 55.2 cm
86.23.66

Door to hallway closet
Oak
76½ x 27½ inches
194.3 x 70 cm
86.23.67

Donald Lovness Cottage

Stillwater, Minnesota, designed 1957,
built 1976

Pair of dining-room chairs originally
designed for Hollyhock House in 1920;
executed for the Lovness house (1976)
Oak, upholstered back and slip-seat,
tassles
Each: 38¼ x 19½ x 10 inches
97.2 x 49.5 x 25.4 cm
86.23.32,33

Donald Lovness House

Stillwater, Minnesota, 1955

Sketches
Pencil on graph paper
8 x 11 inches
20.4 x 28.1 cm
86.23.54

Elevations and details for light fixture, screen and wall
Pencil, colored pencil, and crayon on
paper
Signed "FLW"
December 1958
14 x 36 inches
36.6 x 91.4 cm
86.23.64

Pair of gates
Wrought iron, painted red
Each section: 51½ x 62 x 6 inches
130.8 x 157.5 x 15.2 cm
86.23.68a,b

Darwin D. Martin House

Buffalo, New York, 1904

Two windows
Leaded glass
Each: 58½ x 15⅝ inches
148.6 x 39.7 cm
86.06.04,11

Window
Leaded glass
58⅜ x 24¼ inches
148.9 x 61.6 cm
86.06.10

Window
Leaded glass
35½ x 25¾ inches
90.2 x 65.5 cm
86.08.09

Window
Leaded glass
66⅞ x 28¾ inches
169.8 x 73 cm
86.08.10

Window
Leaded glass in original frame
24½ x 14⅛ inches
62.2 x 35.8 cm
86.20.01

Window
Leaded glass
22¾ x 32⅛ inches
57.8 x 81.7 cm
86.20.02

Window: "Tree of Life"
Leaded glass
39¾ x 27 inches
100.1 x 60 cm
86.31.01

Two windows
Leaded glass
Each: 38⅝ x 18¾ inches
98.1 x 47.6 cm
86.31.02
87.17.13

William E. Martin House

Oak Park, Illinois, 1902

Reclining armchair
Oak
28¾ x 29¼ x 33 inches
73 x 74.3 x 83.8 cm
87.17.12

Midway Gardens

Chicago, Illinois, 1914

Four plates
Glazed porcelain
Each: 6¼ x 9¾ inches
15.8 x 24.8 cm
86.03.01–4

Sprite sculpture
Concrete
71 x 11 x 13 inches
180.3 x 27.9 x 33 cm
86.23.51

Sprite sculpture
Concrete
72 x 15 x 12½ inches
182.9 x 38.1 x 31.8 cm
86.23.52

Sculpture lamp
Concrete
141 x 10½ x 25 inches
358.1 x 26.7 x 63.5 cm
86.23.53

Architectural fragment
Concrete
33 x 27 x 5½ inches
83.8 x 68.6 x 14 cm
86.23.65

Sprite head
Concrete
15 x 10½ x 9 inches
38.1 x 26.7 x 22.9 cm
87.05.01

George Millard House: La Miniatura

Pasadena, California, 1923

Bookcase
Mahogany, felt, gilt
36 x 48 x 3¾ inches
91.4 x 121.9 x 22.2 cm
87.08.01

Nathan G. Moore House

Oak Park, Illinois, 1895

Pair of gates
Wrought iron, painted black
Each section: 74 x 45½ inches
188 x 114.3 cm
88.05.01a,b

New York Exhibition House

New York, New York, 1953

Dismantled house
Cypress, brick, glass, metal
84.01.01

Three clerestory panels
Cypress
Each: 15¾ x 45¾ inches
40 x 116.2 cm
86.02.01–3

Harold C. Price Co. Tower

Bartlesville, Oklahoma, 1953–1956

Side chair
Aluminum, original upholstered seat
and back
32⅝ x 19 x 20¾ inches
82.9 x 48.3 x 52.7 cm
88.06.01

Isabel Roberts House

River Forest, Illinois, 1908

Side chair
Oak, with leather-covered slip-seat
39⅜ x 15 x 17⅝ inches
100 x 38 x 44.7 cm
86.01.06

Frederick C. Robie House

Chicago, Illinois, 1908

Rendering: "Design for glass in basement doors . . . discarded"
Pencil and ink on tracing paper
14¾ x 11¼ inches
37.5 x 28.6 cm
87.17.19

Robert W. Roloson Houses

Chicago, Illinois, 1894

*Window frame, casement sash,
and sub frame*
Oak, with traces of original paint
Framed together: 47⅛ x 49¼ inches
119.7 x 125.1 cm
88.04.01a,b

Mantel and surround
Oak, ceramic tile
Mantel: 63½ x 73¾ x 10 inches
161.3 x 187.3 x 25.4 cm
88.04.02

F. Schumacher & Co.

New York, New York, 1955

Textile (#104)
Printed silk and Fortisan
288 x 49¾ inches
731.5 x 126.4 cm
86.07.01

Textile (#104)
Printed silk and Fortisan
117⅜ x 49¾ inches
298 x 126.4 cm
86.07.02

Textile (#103)
Printed linen
25½ x 47 inches
64.8 x 119.4 cm
86.22.01

Textile (#103)
Printed linen
25½ x 47 inches
64.8 x 119.4 cm
86.22.02

Textile (#403)
Printed linen
25¼ x 23¾ inches
64.1 x 60.4 cm
86.22.03

Textile (#103)
Printed linen
25½ x 47 inches
64.8 x 119.4 cm
86.22.04

Textile (#103)
Printed cotton and Fortisan
24¾ x 45¼ inches
62.8 x 114.9 cm
86.22.05

Textile (#107)
Printed linen
33¼ x 24 inches
84.5 x 61 cm
86.22.06

Textile (#102)
Printed linen
23 x 28 inches
58.4 x 71.1 cm
86.22.07

Textile (#102)
Printed linen
83¾ x 46½ inches
214.5 x 118.1 cm
86.28.01

Sample book: "Schumacher's Taliesin
Line of Decorative Wallpapers"
Printed paper with samples of wallpaper
Closed: 18 x 14¼ inches
45.7 x 36.2 cm
87.01.01

Sample book: "Schumacher's Taliesin
Line of Decorative Fabrics and
Wallpapers"
Printed paper with samples of wallpaper
and fabric
22¾ x 17⅜ inches
57.7 x 44.2 cm
87.03.01

Textile (#103)
Printed linen
90 x 50 inches
228.6 x 127 cm
87.07.01

Talbot Smith House

Ann Arbor, Michigan, 1948

Perspective view of house
Pencil, colored pencil, and ink on
tracing paper
Signed "FLW" and dated "Sept 15/48"
26⅜ x 36⅛ inches
67 x 91.7 cm
86.38.01

Perspective view of house
Pencil, colored pencil, and ink on
tracing paper
Signed "FLW" and dated "Sept 15/48"
26⅜ x 36⅛ inches
67 x 91.7 cm
86.38.02

Plan
Pencil, colored pencil, and ink on
tracing paper
Signed "FLW" and dated "NOV 19/48"
26⅜ x 36⅛ inches
67 x 91.7 cm
86.38.03

Plot plan: house and garage
Pencil, colored pencil, and ink on
tracing paper
Signed "FLW" and dated "Sept 15/48"
26⅜ x 36⅛ inches
67 x 91.7 cm
86.38.04

Set of bound blueprints (eight sheets)
Signed and dated "FLW April 15/49"
With binding: 33¼ x 37 inches
84.5 x 94 cm
86.38.05

Richard C. Smith House

Jefferson, Wisconsin, 1951

Bench
Cypress
15 x 73 x 12½ inches
38.1 x 185.4 x 31.8 cm
86.09.01

Three end tables
Cypress
Each: 10⅛ x 23¾ x 17⅝ inches
25.7 x 60.3 x 44.8 cm
86.09.02–4

Desk
Cypress, brass hardware
25¾ x 57½ x 49½ inches
65.4 x 146.1 x 125.7 cm
86.17.01

End table
Cypress
19⅞ x 20½ inches
50.5 x 52.1 cm
86.17.02

Desk
Cypress
25⅜ x 57⅛ x 49⅞ inches
64.4 x 145.1 x 126.7 cm
86.27.01

Clarence W. Sondern House

Kansas City, Missouri, 1940

Two side chairs
Cypress, with upholstered seat and
back cushions
Each: 28 x 22 x 22¼ inches
71 x 55.9 x 56.5 cm
86.02.04,5

Coffee table
Cypress
18½ x 27¾ x 18⅝ inches
47.2 x 70.8 x 47.5 cm
86.02.06

Side table
Cypress
25⅜ x 30 x 24 inches
64.7 x 76.5 x 61.2 cm
86.02.07a–c

Leigh Stevens House: Auldbrass Plantation

Yemassee, South Carolina, 1940

Center table
Cypress, laminated mahogany core
29½ x 59½ x 59½ inches
74.8 x 151.1 x 151.1 cm
86.05.04

Clerestory panel
Cypress, glass
11½ x 50¼ inches
29.3 x 127.7 cm
86.01.05

Taliesin West

Scottsdale, Arizona, 1938

Armchair, c. 1946
Tropical hardwood, douglas fir, with
upholstered seat and back cushions
Signed "BBB"
30½ x 41⅛ x 36⅝ inches
77.4 x 104.3 x 93 cm
86.01.04

Paul J. Trier House

Des Moines, Iowa, 1956

Side chair
Laminated birch, upholstered seat and
back cushions
37⅛ x 18½ x 19½ inches
94.3 x 47 x 49.5 cm
86.02.08

Coffee table
Birch
18⅛ x 47⅞ x 47⅞ inches
46 x 121.5 x 121.5 cm
86.02.09

Unitarian Church

Sherwood Hills, Wisconsin, 1947

Table
Plywood
25⅛ x 46⅜ x 39⅞ inches
63.8 x 117.8 x 101.3 cm
86.34.11

Bench
Plywood, upholstered back and seat
cushions, chain
27½ x 42 x 22⅞ inches
69.8 x 106.7 x 58.1 cm
86.34.12

Chair
Plywood, upholstered back and seat
cushions, chain
27¾ x 20¾ x 23⅝ inches
70.5 x 52.7 x 60 cm
86.34.13

Bench
Plywood, upholstered back and seat
cushions, chain
27¾ x 20¾ x 24½ inches
70.5 x 52.7 x 62.2 cm
86.34.14

Charles E. Weltzheimer House

Oberlin, Ohio, 1948

Clerestory panel
Oak
11⅜ x 47⅜ inches
28.9 x 120.3 cm
85.02.08

Ward W. Willits House

Highland Park, Illinois, 1902

Side chair
Oak, with leather-covered slip-seat
55¾ x 17 x 18 inches
141.5 x 43.3 x 45.8 cm
86.34.10

Wright Home and Studio

Oak Park, Illinois, 1889, 1893, 1895

Urn, designed c. 1895–1900
Probably used in this commission
Sheet copper
17½ x 19⅛ x 19⅛ inches
44.5 x 48.5 x 48.5 cm
86.24.01

Two vases, designed c. 1895–1900
Probably used in this commission
Sheet copper
Each: 28 x 4¼ x 4¼ inches
71.1 x 10.9 x 10.9 cm
86.26.01,2

GRAPHICS AND BOOKS DESIGNED BY FRANK LLOYD WRIGHT

(Listed chronologically)

William C. Gannet
The House Beautiful
Published by the Auvergne Press,
River Forest, Illinois
1897
Closed: 14 x 11¾ inches
35.6 x 29.8 cm
86.23.95

Frank Lloyd Wright
*Ausgeführte Bauten und Entwürfe von
Frank Lloyd Wright* 1st edition
Published by Ernst Wasmuth, Berlin
1910
86.08.07a vol 1
86.08.07b vol 2

Frank Lloyd Wright
*Ausgeführte Bauten und Entwürfe von
Frank Lloyd Wright* 1st edition
Published by Ernst Wasmuth, Berlin
1910
86.23.50a vol 1
86.23.50b vol 2

Special issues of Wendingen, "The Life-
Work of the American Architect
Frank Lloyd Wright"
Published by C.A. Mees, Santpoort,
Holland
1925
Each: 13⅜ x 13 inches
34 x 33 cm
86.23.93a (complete set)
86.23.93b–e (miscellaneous numbers)

Designs for *Liberty* magazine covers, c. 1927

Drawing: *January, The Frozen Sphere*
Pencil and crayon on paper
Signed "FLW"
13½ x 23½ inches
34.3 x 59.7 cm
86.08.02

Drawing: *February, The Jeweler's Window*
Pencil and crayon on paper
Signed "FLW"
14¼ x 24 inches
36.2 x 60.1 cm
86.29.02

Drawing: *March, Balloons*
Pencil and crayon on paper
Signed "FLW"
14³⁄₁₆ x 24 inches
36 x 60.1 cm
86.08.01

Drawing: *April, Showers*
Pencil and crayon on paper
Signed "FLW"
14⅛ x 24 inches
35.9 x 60.1 cm
86.29.01

Drawing: *June, The Garden Window*
Pencil and crayon on paper
Signed "FLW"
14 x 23⅞ inches
35.6 x 60 cm
86.29.03

Drawing: *December*—Untitled
Pencil and crayon on paper
14⅛ x 24¼ inches
35.9 x 61.6 cm
86.08.03

Frank Lloyd Wright
An Autobiography 1st edition
Published by Longmans, Green and
Company
1932
Closed: 9⅛ x 7½ inches
23.2 x 19 cm
86.23.100

Town and Country
July 1937
13½ x 9¾ inches
34.3 x 24.7 cm
86.23.106

Frank Lloyd Wright
Architectural Forum
January 1938
Closed: 12 x 9¼ inches
30.5 x 23.5 cm
86.23.108

Frank Lloyd Wright
An Autobiography 2nd edition
Published by Duell, Sloan and Pearce,
New York
1943
Closed 9⅛ x 7½ inches
23.2 x 19 cm
86.23.99

OTHER DESIGNERS
& MANUFACTURERS

(Listed alphabetically by designer)

Adler and Sullivan (working 1883–1895)

Chicago, Illinois

Auditorium Building
Chicago, Illinois, 1886–1889

Window
Colored and textured glass in original
frame
31 x 52⅝ inches
78.7 x 133.7 cm
86.37.01

Chicago Stock Exchange Building
Chicago, Illinois, 1893

Elevator grille
Wrought iron
74 x 58⅝ inches
188 x 148.9 cm
87.10.01

Elevator frieze
Cast iron, copper plated
18 x 67½ x 3⅝ inches
45.7 x 171.5 x 9.1 cm
87.10.02

Schiller Building (later known as the Garrick Building)
Chicago, Illinois, 1891

Block
Terra-cotta
13⅛ x 12 x 11⅞ inches
33.4 x 30.5 x 30.2 cm
87.04.01

Block
Terra-cotta
16¾ x 12 x 11⅞ inches
42.5 x 30.5 x 30.2 cm
87.04.02

Block
Terra-cotta
12¾ x 12 x 11⅞ inches
32.4 x 30.5 x 30.1 cm
87.04.03

American Terra Cotta Company

Terra Cotta, Illinois, 1900–1910

Vase
Glazed earthenware
"TECO" impressed twice on bottom
6¾ x 3 (diameter) inches
17.1 x 7.6 cm
88.07.01

Vase
Glazed earthenware
"TECO" impressed on bottom
10⅞ x 4½ (diameter) inches
27.6 x 11.4 cm
88.07.02

Vase
Glazed earthenware
On bottom: "TECO" impressed,
"297" incised
5½ x 8¾ x 5¾ inches
14 x 22.2 x 14.6 cm
88.07.03

Vase
Glazed earthenware
On bottom: "TECO" impressed,
"73" incised.
25¹⁄₁₆ x 7¹¹⁄₁₆ (diameter) inches
63.7 x 19.5 cm
88.07.04

Christopher Dresser (1834–1904)

London, England

Plate, c. 1886
Glazed earthenware
9¹⁄₁₆ (diameter) inches
23 cm
87.18.01

William E. Drummond (1876–1946)

Thorncroft
Riverside, Illinois, 1909

Two armchairs
Oak, leather upholstery
35¼ x 31⅜ x 27¼ inches
89.5 x 79.7 x 69.2 cm
85.02.05,6

Couch
Oak, leather upholstery
28 x 187½ x 31 inches
71.1 x 476.3 x 78.7 cm
85.02.07

William Morris (1834–1896)

London, England

Textile, late nineteenth century
Printed cotton
20 x 20 inches
51 x 51 cm
87.19.01

George M. Niedecken (1878–1945)

E. P. Irving House (designed by Frank Lloyd
Wright, completed by Herman V.
von Holst 1874–1955)
Decatur, Illinois, 1910

Table and couch ensemble
Oak, upholstered seat and back cushion
33½ x 77 x 60⅝ inches
85.1 x 195.6 x 154 cm
86.32.01

Thomas Olson (b. 1930)

(Site Supervisor, office of
Frank Lloyd Wright)

Gerald B. Tonkens House (designed by
Frank Lloyd Wright)
Cincinnati, Ohio, 1954

Cat house
Painted wood
48⅜ x 47¾ x 50 inches
123 x 121.5 x 126 cm
87.17.20

*Elevations, sections, perspective of a house
for a pet cat*
Colored pencil and pen on paper
19½ x 32¾ inches
49.5 x 83.2 cm
87.17.21

Charles Rohlfs (1853–1936)

Buffalo, New York

Side chair, c. 1902
Mahogany
Stamped on bottom of seat, "R/1902"
43⅜ x 18⅝ x 20⅛ inches
110.2 x 47.3 x 51.1 cm
88.08.01

Gustav Stickley (1857–1946)

Eastwood, New York

Rocker, c. 1905
Oak, original leather upholstery
Stamped on stretcher, "Als ik kan/
Stickley"
41⁷⁄₁₆ x 17½ x 28 inches
105.3 x 44.4 x 71.1 cm
86.34.01

Louis H. Sullivan (1856–1924)

Chicago, Illinois

Henry C. Adams Building
Algona, Iowa, 1913

Pair of urns
Glazed terra-cotta
Each: 12¾ x 36¼ (diameter) inches
32.4 x 92.1 cm
86.03.01,2

Guaranty Building
Buffalo, New York, 1894–1895

Two door escutcheons, including door
handles and front and back plates
Cast iron
Each: 14⅜ x 4⅛ x 7½ inches
36.5 x 10.5 x 19.1 cm
86.23.76a,b

Two stair balusters
Cast iron, copper plated
Each: 48 x 14 inches
121.9 x 35.6 cm
86.23.77,78

Two floor plates
Cast iron, copper plated
Each: 11¾ x 12¾ inches
29.8 x 32.4 cm
86.23.79,80

Two elevator panels with escutcheons
Cast iron, copper plate
Each: 72 x 12¾ inches
182.9 x 32.4 cm
86.23.81,2

Two elevator frieze panels
Cast iron, copper plated
Each: 11¾ x 88¾ inches
29.8 x 225.4 cm
86.23.83a,b

Elevator frieze panel
Cast iron, copper plated
17¼ x 52 inches
44.8 x 132.1 cm
86.23.84a

Elevator frieze panel
Cast iron, copper plated
90⅜ x 7 inches
229.5 x 17.8 cm
86.23.84b

National Farmers' Bank
Owatonna, Minnesota, 1906–1908

Ceiling ornament
Glazed terra-cotta
10½ x 22¼ x 9⅞ inches
26.7 x 56.5 x 25.1 cm
86.23.75

Wicket: reproduction
Bronze
40¼ x 22½ inches
102.2 x 57.2 cm
86.23.85

Tiffany Studios (working 1902–1932)

New York, New York

Table lamp
Shade, leaded glass
Base, glazed earthenware made by
Grueby Faience Company, Boston
(working 1894–1911)
1902–1911
Paper label on bottom: "GRUEBY
POTTERY/BOSTON USA REG. TRADEMARK"
21½ x 15¾ (diameter) inches
54.6 x 40 cm
87.17.01

APPENDIX

Guidelines for Collecting the
Decorative Designs of Frank Lloyd Wright

Based on the recommendations of The Domino's Pizza Preservation Committee, the following guidelines have been adopted by The National Center for the Study of Frank Lloyd Wright for The Domino's Pizza Collection.

–Domino's does not purchase objects, especially windows and built-in furniture, directly from Wright homeowners.

–When offered Wright-designed objects, Domino's makes careful inquiries into provenance to ascertain that the objects were not removed illegally.

–If offered Wright-designed objects from a house that is now a museum, Domino's gives the institution the opportunity to acquire the object first.

–Domino's makes an effort to return (by sale, gift, or loan) Wright-designed objects original to buildings that are now museums.

–Domino's permits owners of Wright buildings to have access to artifacts in The Domino's Pizza Collection for the purpose of one-time only reproductions, to encourage authentic restorations. A statement is required guaranteeing that the reproduction will be "one-time only" for use in the restoration of a specific house. Reproductions must be permanently labeled as such.

–If the deteriorating condition of original architectural elements of a Wright structure necessitates their removal, Domino's makes every effort to direct these architectural elements to museum collections. Where there is duplicate material, we encourage interested museums to share in preserving these architectural elements.

–Domino's encourages owners of Wright buildings to maintain the architectural integrity of both the interior and exterior of their structures. Domino's encourages renovations for the convenience of contemporary living to be undertaken with sensitivity and, whenever possible, with the professional advice of a qualified restoration architect. The removal of windows, etc., in any restoration should be documented, and the artifacts stored in the house or lent to a museum.

SELECT BIBLIOGRAPHY

This bibliography is divided into two sections. The first includes general works that contain information on almost every project discussed in this book. The second section includes publications that pertain to specific commissions.

GENERAL BOOKS

Futagawa, Yukio, ed., and Bruce Brooks Pfeiffer, text. *Frank Lloyd Wright* Vols. 1–12. Tokyo: ADA Edita, 1984–8.

Hanks, David A. *The Decorative Designs of Frank Lloyd Wright*. New York: E. P. Dutton, 1979.

Hitchcock, Henry Russell. *In the Nature of Materials: 1887–1941, the Buildings of Frank Lloyd Wright*. New York: Duell, Sloan and Pearce, 1942.

Manson, Grant Carpenter. *Frank Lloyd Wright to 1910: The First Golden Age*. New York: Van Nostrand Reinhold Co., 1958.

Meehan, Patrick J. *Frank Lloyd Wright: A Research Guide to Archival Sources*. New York: Garland, 1983.

Storrer, William Allin. *The Architecture of Frank Lloyd Wright: A Complete Catalogue*. Cambridge, Mass.: MIT Press, 1974.

Sweeney, Robert. *Frank Lloyd Wright: An Annotated Bibliography*. Los Angeles: Hennessey and Ingalls, 1978.

Wright, Frank Lloyd. *In the Cause of Architecture: Essays by Frank Lloyd Wright for Architectural Record 1908–1952*. Edited by Frederick Gutheim. New York: Architectural Record, 1975.

COMMISSIONS

Barnsdall, Aline

Levine, Neil. "Landscape into Architecture: Frank Lloyd Wright's Hollyhock House and the Romance of Southern California." *AA Files. Annals of the Architectural Association School of Architecture* 3 (July 1983): 22–41.

Smith, Kathryn. "Frank Lloyd Wright, Hollyhock House and Olive Hill, 1914–1924." *Journal of the Society of Architectural Historians* 38 (March 1979): 15–33.

Coonley, Avery

"A Departure from Classic Tradition: Two Unusual Houses by Louis Sullivan and Frank Lloyd Wright." *Architectural Record* 30 (October 1911): 326–338.

Dana, Susan

Cavanaugh, Tom R., and Payne E. L. Thomas. *A Frank Lloyd Wright House: Bannerstone House, Springfield, Illinois*. Springfield, Illinois: Charles C. Thomas, [1970].

Slaton, Deborah, and Harry J. Hunderman. *The Dana Thomas House.* Vol. 1, *Historic Structures Report.* Vol. 2, *Furniture Inventory.* Vol. 3, *Art Glass Inventory.* Prepared for the Illinois Historic Preservation Agency and Capitol Development Board. Chicago: Hasbrouck Hunderman Architects, 1984–1985.

Greene, William B.

Eaton, Leonard K. "Mr. and Mrs. William Greene (Aurora, Illinois, 1912)." In *Two Chicago Architects and Their Clients*, 98–111. Cambridge, Mass.: MIT Press, 1969.

Heller, Joseph

Spencer, Robert C., Jr. "The Work of Frank Lloyd Wright." *Architectural Review* 7 (June 1900): 61–72.

Spencer, Robert C., Jr. "Brick Architecture In and About Chicago." *Brickbuilder* 12 (September 1903): 178–187.

Heritage-Henredon

"Frank Lloyd Wright Designs Home Furnishings You Can Buy!" *House Beautiful* 97 (November 1955): 282–290, 336–341.

Hillside Home School

Bohrer, Florence Fifer. "The Unitarian Hillside Home School." *Wisconsin Magazine of History* 38 (September 1955): 151–155.

Husser, Joseph

Strauss, Irma. "Husser House Dining Room Set." *The Frank Lloyd Wright Newsletter* 2 (First Quarter 1979): 5–9.

Imperial Hotel

"Committee for the Preservation of the Imperial Hotel." *Inland Architect* 11 (December 1967): 12–13.

James, Cary. *The Imperial Hotel: Frank Lloyd Wright and the Architecture of Unity.* Rutland, Vt., and Tokyo: Charles E. Tuttle Company, [1968].

Kostka, Robert. "Frank Lloyd Wright in Japan." *Prairie School Review* 3 (Third Quarter 1966): 5–23 and cover.

Smith, Kathryn. "Frank Lloyd Wright and the Imperial Hotel: A Postscript." *Art Bulletin* 67 (June 1985): 296–310.

Stone, Jabez K. "The Monument: The Most Talked about Hotel in the World; Tokyo's Unique Survival of Disaster." *Japan* 13 (January 1924): 13–17, 37, 40–41, 43, 45.

Sullivan, Louis H. "Concerning the Imperial Hotel, Tokyo, Japan." *Architectural Record* 53 (April 1923): 332–352.

Watanabe, Yoshio, photographer, and Tachu Naito, Shindo Akashi, and Gakujii Yamamoto, text. *Imperial Hotel 1921–67.* Tokyo: Kajima Institute Publishing Company, 1968.

Kaufmann, Edgar

Hoffman, Donald. *Frank Lloyd Wright's Fallingwater: The House and its History.* New York: Dover, 1978.

Kaufmann, Edgar, jr. *Fallingwater, A Frank Lloyd Wright Country House.* New York: Cross River Press, 1986.

New York. Museum of Modern Art. *A New House by Frank Lloyd Wright on Bear Run, Pennsylvania.* New York: The Museum of Modern Art, 1938.

Larkin Building

Berlage, H.P. "The New American Architecture." In *The Literature of Architecture: The Evolution of Architectural Theory and Practice in Nineteenth-Century America*, edited by Don Gifford. New York: E.P. Dutton, 1966.

Puma, Jerome. "The Larkin Building, Buffalo, New York: History of the Demolition." *Frank Lloyd Wright Newsletter* 1 (September–October 1978): 2–7.

Quinan, Jack. *Frank Lloyd Wright's Larkin Building. Myth and Fact.* Cambridge, Mass.: MIT Press, 1987.

Sturgis, Russell. "The Larkin Building in Buffalo." *Architectural Record* 23 (April 1908): 310–321.

Twitmyer, Geo. E. "A Model Administration Building." *Business Man's Magazine* 19 (April 1907): 43–49.

Little Houses

Haight, Deborah S., and Pete F. Blume. *Frank Lloyd Wright: The Library from the Francis W. Little House.* Allentown, Pa.: Allentown Art Museum, 1978.

Heckscher, Morrison, and Elizabeth G. Miller. *An Architect and His Client: Frank Lloyd Wright and Francis W. Little.* New York: The Metropolitan Museum of Art, May 2, 1973.

Heckscher, Morrison. "Frank Lloyd Wright's Furniture for Francis W. Little." *Burlington Magazine* 117 (December 1975): 871–872.

Johnson, Kathryn C. "Frank Lloyd Wright and the Strong-Minded Littles." *Architecture Minnesota* 7 (October–November 1981): 52–57.

Johnson, Kathryn C. "Frank Lloyd Wright's Mature Prairie Style." *Minneapolis Institute of Arts Bulletin* 61 (1974): 54–65.

Martin, Darwin D.

Berlage, H.P. "The New American Architecture." In *The Literature of Architecture: The Evolution of Architectural Theory and Practice in Nineteenth-Century America*, edited by Don Gifford. New York: E.P. Dutton, 1966.

Licht, Ira. "Stained Glass Panels of Frank Lloyd Wright." *Arts Magazine* 43 (November 1968): 34–35.

"Masterpieces of Two Sullivan Students: One Is Destroyed, One Saved." *Architectural Record* 147 (April 1970): 40.

Menocal, Narciso G., "Form and Content in Frank Lloyd Wright's *Tree of Life* Window." *Elvehjem Museum of Art Bulletin* (University of Wisconsin-Madison 1984): 18–32.

"Wright's Martin House to Be Restored." *Progressive Architecture* 48 (November 1967): 63.

Midway Gardens

Fern, Alan M. "The Midway Gardens of Frank Lloyd Wright." *Architectural Review* 134 (August 1963): 113–116.

Moore, Nathan

[Chicago Architectural Club.] *Annual of the Chicago Architectural Club, Being the Book of the Thirteenth Annual Exhibition 1900.* Chicago: Architectural Club, 1900.

Spencer, Robert C., Jr. "The Work of Frank Lloyd Wright." *Architectural Review* 7 (June 1900): 61–72.

Price Tower

De Long, David. "A Tower Expressive of Unique Interiors." *AIA Journal* 71 (July 1982): 78–83.

"18-Story Tower Cantilever Structure of Concrete and Glass: Dramatic Frank Lloyd Wright Design." *Building Materials Digest* 14 (December 1954): 425.

"Frank Lloyd Wright: After 36 Years His Tower Is Completed." *Architectural Forum* 104 (February 1956): 106–113 and cover.

"Frank Lloyd Wright's Concrete and Copper Skyscraper on the Prairie for H.C. Price Co." *Architectural Forum* 98 (May 1953): 98–105 and cover.

"The H.C. Price Tower." *Architectural Record* 119 (February 1956): 153–160 and cover.

The Price Tower. Architect: Frank Lloyd Wright. Bartlesville, Okla.: H.C. Price Co., 1956.

Wright, Frank Lloyd. *The Story of the Tower: The Tree that Escaped the Crowded Forest.* New York: Horizon Press, 1956.

"Wright Completes Skyscraper." *Progressive Architecture* 37 (February 1956): 87–90.

Schumacher

"Frank Lloyd Wright; A Master Architect Creates Fabric and Wallpaper Designs." *American Fabrics and Fashions* 35 (Winter 1955–56): 50–51.

"New Era for Wright at 86: The Marketplace Redeemed?" *Architectural Record* 118 (October 1955): 20.

"Schumacher's Taliesin Line of Decorative Fabrics and Wallpapers." (Sample Book) Schumacher, 1955.

"Schumacher's Taliesin Line of Decorative Wallpapers" (Sample Book) Schumacher, 1955.

Stephens, Leigh

Stamm, Gunther. "Modern Architecture and the Plantation Nostalgia of the 1930s: Stone's 'Mepkin' and Wright's 'Auldbrass Plantation.'" *Journal of the Society of Architectural Historians* 34 (December 1975): 318.

Unity Temple

Bowly, Devereux, Jr. "Unity Temple, a Masterpiece on the Way to Restoration." *Inland Architect* 16 (December 1972): 18.

Johonnot, Dr. Rodney F. *The New Edifice of Unity Church, Frank Lloyd Wright. Descriptive and Historical Matter.* [Oak Park, Illinois]: The New Unity Church Club, 1906.

"Preservation: Fund Drive Launched to Complete Restoration of Unity Temple." *AIA Journal* 68 (January 1979): 32.

Slaton, Deborah, and Harry J. Hunderman. *Unity Temple Historic Structures Report.* Prepared for the Unity Temple Restoration Foundation, Oak Park, Illinois. Chicago: Wiss, Janney, Elstner Associates, 1987.

"Unity Restored." *Architectural Review* 131 (January 1962): 5–6.

Wright, Henry. "Unity Temple, Oak Park, Illinois." *Architectural Forum* 130 (June 1969): 28–37 and cover.

Usonian Exhibition House

"Frank Lloyd Wright Builds in the Middle of Manhattan, Shows How to Make a Small, Simple House Rich and Spacious." *House and Home* 4 (November 1953): 118–121.

[Wright, Frank Lloyd.] *The Usonian House, Souvenir of the Exhibition: 60 Years of Living Architecture, the Work of Frank Lloyd Wright.* [New York]: The Solomon R. Guggenheim Museum, [1953].

Wall, Carlton D.

"Frank Lloyd Wright in Michigan." *AIA Monthly Bulletin. Michigan Society of Architects* 33 (December 1959): 17–32 and cover.

Willits, Ward

Linch, Mark David. "The Ward Willits House." *Frank Lloyd Wright Newsletter* 2 (Second Quarter 1979): 1–5.

"Plan for Wright's Willits House Denied by Illinois City Council." *AIA Journal* 72 (December 1983): 18.

Photograph Credits

The Art Institute of Chicago: p. 72

Leonard Eaton: p. 82

P. E. Guerrero: p. 110

David A. Hanks & Associates, Inc.: p. 71, 114

Hedrich-Blessing: Frontispiece, p. 100

Henry Russell Hitchcock: p. 26, 28, 30

Balthazar Korab: p. 10, 12, 14, 19

The Library of Congress, p. 61

Mr. S. D. Loring: p. 105

Donald and Virginia Lovness: p. 120

The Metropolitan Museum of Art: p. 34, 57

The National Center for the Study of Frank Lloyd Wright:
p. 20, 24, 102, 106

   Gregg Campbell: p. 23, 25, 33, 35, 37, 39, 40, 41, 42, 43, 44, 45,
   47, 48, 50, 51, 52, 54, 55, 56, 58, 59, 60, 65, 68, 69, 70, 76, 77,
   78, 79, 83, 85, 87, 88, 93, 94, 95, 97, 98, 101, 103, 104, 109, 111,
   112, 113, 115, 116, 117, 119, 121, 122, 123, 125, 126, 127, 128,
   129, 133

   Chicago Architectural Photographic Co. Collection: p. 22, 34,
   36, 38, 62, 64, 66, 74, 81, 86, 89, 90, 92

   Suzanne Coles: Front and Back cover, 27, 49, 53, 67, 131

   Richard P. Goodbody: p. 29

   Brian Howard: p. 31

   Andy Sacks: p. 63, 73, 80, 91, 107

The Wright Collection, Spencer Library, University of Kansas,
Lawrence: p. 93, 118

Mrs. Raymond V. Stevenson: p. 84

Ezra Stoller at ESTO: p. 96, 99

The Frank Lloyd Wright Memorial Foundation: p. 108

INDEX

Page numbers in boldface indicate illustrations